Marriages
of
Hancock County
Georgia
- 1806-1850 -

Compiled By:
Martha Lou Houston

Southern Historical Press, Inc.
Greenville, South Carolina

SOUTHERN HISTORICAL PRESS, INC.
PO BOX 1267
Greenville, SC   29601

ISBN #978-1-63914-058-9

Printed in the United States of America

STATE OF GEORGIA

HANCOCK COUNTY

Attached is an exact copy of an INDEX to the Marriage Records of Hancock County 1806-1850 inclusive, this index being the personal property of the under-signed. The original record carries the date of issuance of license, the names of the contracting parties, the place of residence of each, and date of execution and the name of the person performing the ceremony. For example:

"Dec. 17 1806 Lemuel Pruitt of Warren County & Jane R. Sutton of Hancock 18 Dec 1806 by Wingate Hall   J.P."

In testimony whereof, I have hereunto set my hand and affixed the Seal of the Court of Ordinary this the 16th day of October, 1946.

Mildred L. Brantley Ordinary

CONTRACTING PARTIES	MARRIAGE DATE
Alford, Robert & Mason	12-23-1806
Armstrong, Mackey & Elizabeth Veazey	12-25-1806
Amerson, Uriah & Elizabeth Rachels	8-30-1807
Averett, Drury & Elizabeth Smith	No date
Ashhurst, Robert & Mary Mangham	No date
Andrews, William & Betheny Mason	12-22-1808
Arnold, Reason & Sophia Waller	1-3- 1809
Allen, Drury & Milly Whitehurst	10-24-1807
Averett, Benjamin & Patsy Walker	4-20-1809
Adams, Reubin & Burchett Lloyd	No date
Allen, Berry & Zilphey Barnes	2- 5- 1810
Ashley, John & Charity Veazey	11-30-1809
Andrews, William & Betsey Goodwin	4-28-1811
Alfriend, Edward D. & Nancy Hamilton	12- 3-1811
Andrews, William & Betsey Goodwin(See Above)	4-28-1811
Archer, William & Giddy Harris	10-17-1811
Allen, William & Phereby Horton	12-24-1812
Andrews, Marcus & Ann Connell	No date
Andrews, Robert & Eliza Norsworthy	No date
Andrews, Dr. Moses & Mary M. Chambers	4-11-1815
Adams, Robert & Frances Hudson	No date
Arnold, Jehu & Vicy Peavy	12-31-1815
Alford, Jacob & Martha Culver	2- 2-1818
Alexander, Nathaniel G. & Mary Mapp	No date
Allen, George & Cassey Eubanks	10-12-1820

Arnold, Willie & Elviry Loyd	12-14-1820
Andrews, Samuel R. & Sarah Ransom	No date
Allen, Charles & Sarah H. Denby	1-20-1821
Allen, James A. & Elizabeth Duckworth	1-30-1821
Aspinewall, George & Elizabeth Eleanor Butts	3-13-1823
Audas, Tuttle H. & Mary A. S. Turner	No date
Akins, Thomas & Caroline Reynolds	5-29-1823
Arnold, Peter & Narcissa Frazer	1-11-1824
Albritton, Lanier & Mrs. Martha Holson Bake	4-29-1824
Audas, Tuttle H. & Henrietta W. Turner	9-22-1824
Akins, John & Hixsey Harris	12-21-1824
Allen, Parham & Elizabeth Ann Spencer	2-24-1825
Alexander, Asa C. & Mrs. Pheriba Kendall	4-21-1825
Askew, Uriah & Elizabeth R. Askew	12-29-1825
Averitt, Albrit & Jane Cook	2-8-1826
Alfriend, Abram & Sarah H. Hall	11-19-1826
Allen, Tillman B. & Maria Killgore	No date
Ausburn, George &Tuvinah McDaniel	10-9-1827
Allen, Edmund & Rebecca Williams	12-27-1827
Archer, Elias & Elizabeth Gilbert	12-23-1828
Averitt, Albutt & Mary Vinson	1-1-1829
Archer, James & Mariah Norris	12-30-1828
Askew, William & Mary Gerald	No date
Amoss, Daniel J. & Caroline J. Harper	9-30-1829
Allen, James & Mary Johnson	No date
Arnold, William Jr. & Martha Ann Marshall	3-23-1830
Alford, Obadiah & Martha Saunders	10-10-1827

Amoss, George W. & Catharine Hamack.	4-24-1831
Andrews, Edwin R. & Mary Ann McKinley Haynes	6-21-1831
Allen, Jackson & Lucy B. Seales	12-7-1831
Archer, Williamson & Mary P. Simpson	October 1832
Akins, Jacob C. & Elizabeth Brewer	3-7-1833
Archer, William Jr. & Elizabeth Jackson	8-1-1833
Amerson, Britain & Eliza Barnes	No date
Archer, Asa & Delitha H. Garland	12-5-1833
Askew, James P. & Maria T. Connell	5-15-1834
Alford, Almon B. & Harriett Eubanks	8-13-1835
Amerson, Barney & Louisa Cobb	9-6-1835
Askew, William & Ann G. Reed	No date
Askew, James & Ann Daniel	11-26-1835
Arnold, Nathaniel & Lucinda Durakin	2-7-1836
Albritton, Joel & Cassandra A. Youngblood	1-14-1836
Ashurs, John T. & Phoebe Ann Bishop	9-31-1836
Arnold, Jesse & Martha Gordy	No date
Amerson, Britain & Kesiah Culver	5-15-1837
Amos, Beverly & Mary E. Butts	12-27-1837
Atkinson, Elbert & Mrs. Elizabeth A. Hixon	2-4-1838
Archer, Tilman T. & Emily Mitchell	10-9-1838
Archer, Alexander & Elizabeth Mitchell	11-7-1838
Alford, Hamlin C. & Emily A. Howell	4-13-1841
Askew, John & Mrs. Sarah Maria Grigsby	6-7-1841
Amos, Henry D. & Mary A. Walker	9-9-1841
Alford, John L. & Susan H. Temple	10-12-1841
Andrews, John W. & Martha E. Hilsman	11-23-1841

Ashley, Josiah & Julia Ann Humphrey	11-25-1841
Ashfield, Virgil & Rebecca Caldwell	No date
Arnold, Everett & Mary Stewart	7-25-1843
Amoss, William & Rebecca B. Latimer	2-25-1845
Amoss, John & Eliza C. Harper	5-17-1845
Anthony, Dr. Joseph George & Mary Elizabeth Thomas	5-4-1846
Andrews, John D. Esq. & Louisa F. Griggs	8-4-1846
Amerson, John & Frances Griffis	7-28-1846
Arnold, Obediah & Elizabeth J. Strother	10-21-1848
Armstrong, John & Mrs. Roxana White	12-11-1849
Armstrong, Anthony C. & Rachel Ann Bowers	1-9-1850
Allen, Wm. M. & Margaret E. Cason	11-7-1850
Blankenship, David & Jency Ellis	No date
Barksdale, Joseph & Ann Holt	11-27-1806
Bailey, John & Nancy Bledsoe	4-23-1807
Butts, Samuel & Eliza Lucas	11-2-1807
Bartlett, Starling & Betsey Archer	12-24-1807
Barnett, Douglas & Mary Todd	7-28-1808
Bell, Samuel & Betsey Gilbert	4-24-1806
Bags, Joseph & Polly Benson	5-4-1806
Beggam, Joseph & Ann Ware	5-22-1806
Barnes, Abel & Isabella Allen	10-6-1808
Barksdale, William & Nancy Long	No date
Bulluke, Joseph & Elizabeth Brantley	12-29-1808
Bishop, Purnal & Elizabeth Dent	No date
Blount, Granberry & Sarah Miller	No date
Brantley, William & Mrs. Ann Martin	9-14-1809
Biggam, Francis & Peggy Hall	9-22-1809

Brown, John & Fanny Duprey	No date
Brown, Larken & Sally Cooper	2-12-1810
Bass, Burwell & Betsey Harper	2-8-1810
Bask, John T. & Elizabeth Bazor	1-17-1810
Bagby, James & Sarah Maddox	6-9-1810
Bazor, William & Polly Layfield	5-20-1810
Brown, Robert & Patsy Hall	7-15-1810
Borland, John & Mary Mathis	11-1-1810
Bishop, Reubin & Polly Hamilton	11-26-1810
Burnley, Richmond & Sally Veazey	12-27-1810
Barksdale, William F. & Rosanna Smith	No date
Burch, Girard & Susannah Simms	1-22-1811
Blanton, Benjamin & Susannah Rountree	7-8-1811
Beckam, John & Susan Davis	7-15-1811
Brown, John & Joanah Armstrong	1-2-1812
Baker, Jesse & Polly Beach	1-16-1812
Bradford, Nathaniel & Sally Temple	2-2-1812
Barksdale, Daniel & Phebe H. Pruitt	3-1-1812
Bray, Benjamin & Louisa Blount	9-29-1812
Barnhart, Geo. & Rhoda Goar	8-27-1812
Bryley, Shadrake & Polly Brantley	7-24-1812
Brantley, James & Sally Binum	2-14-1813
Bray, Benjamin & Vicy Walters	9-24-1813
Barnes, Jesse & Nancy Culver	6-3-1813
Blair, Richey & Synthia Smith	11-5-1813
Benjamin, John David Collins & Kizia Foster	6-29-1814
Bird, Richard & Mary Goodwin	11-10-1814
Bray, Peter & Jincy Peace	2-5-1815

Battle, Jesse B. & Martha Rabun	2-23-1815
Barnes, Benjamin & Amey Williamson	6-25-1815
Brown, Hiram & Sirinia Collins	5-30-1814
Bynum, John & Susannah Jackson	7-18-1815
Brown, William & Elizabeth Wilson	10-4-1815
Butler, David & Frances W. Shackleford	1-18-1816
Bradford, Timothy & Deannah Ray	1-25-1816
Bryant, John & Catharine Jones	1-18-1816
Belcher, Littleton & Lucindy Smith	4-4-1816
Blake, Benjamin & Lucy I. Mitchell	11-28-1816
Barnes, George & Elizabeth Lewis	12-34-1816
Breedlove, Richard & Sarah Wayne	1-9-1817
Butts, Thomas C. & Elizabeth A. Edwards	1-14-1817
Burt, Robert & Dorothy Lewis	6-5-1813
Brown, Jesse S. & Nancy Haswell	6-22-1817
Brown, Edmund & Anna Goare	No date
Breedlove, William & Anna Wayne	7-30-1817
Burch, Jared Jr. & Betsey H. Beckham	8-7-1817
Berry, John & Malinda Turner	8-15-1817
Buttridge, Joseph & Ann Wallace	8-17-1817
Binges, Joseph & Polly Skinner	9-25-1817
Brazil, Mansfield & Nancy H. (?)	10-20-1817
Barksdale, William C. & Mrs. Martha Adams	10-7-1817
Burgamy, Robert & Charon Moore	10-23-1817
Butts, James & Elizabeth Ann Lucas	11-5-1817
Barnes, Abel & Elizabeth Dennis	11-26-1817
Brown, Pressley & Nancy Buckner	2-24-1818
Brown, William & Amey Warren	6-21-1818

Brown, John S. & Lucretia Maddox	7-9-1818
Brown, William & Syntha L. Benson	10-29-1818
Brown B.(?) & Martha Shackleford	11-5-1818
Brady, Mills L. & Elizabeth Jones	4-1-1819
Bonner, Pleasant & Elizabeth R. Mathis	5-4-1819
Battle, Dr. Andrews & Caroline M. Duggar	No date
Broadnax, Robert & Nancy Carmean	9-1-1819
Barnes, William & Sarah Allen	11-23-1819
Brown, William F. & Mrs. Mary Biggins	12-16-1819
Baxter, Eli H. & Julia Richardson	12-21-1819
Brown, Burwell & Elizabeth Griggs	No date
Barnes, James & Elizabeth Johnson	2-10-1820
Black, Peter & Mary Griggs	4-27-1820
Brooking, Robert N. & Martha R. Clayborn	5-18-1820
Buckner, Morris & Rebecca Youngblood	5-13-1820
Belden, Nelson S. & Catharine E. Childers	5-30-1820
Brimberry, John & Mary Archer	5-28-1820
Bradley, Spier & Elizabeth Crimaen	5-31-1820
Butts, Math C. & Sarah S. Stebbins	6-20-1820
Brimberry, George Anderson & Nancy Morris	12-5-1820
Barnes, Lewis B. & Linnah Griggs	12-19-1820
Black, Ryel & Sarah Brimberry	1-26-1821
Breedlove, William W. & Lucy Warren	3-6-1812
Beman, Nathan S. S. & Caroline Yancy	4-3-1821
Brown, Nathaniel & Rebecca Danforth	No date
Burch, Richard C. & Martha Jernigan	3-6-1822
Burnet, James H. & Sarah C. Tucker	5-5-1822
Bickers, Jonathon & Elizabeth Champion	5-5-1822

Blankenship, Solomon & Frankie Kilgore	5-25-1822
Buckner, Appleton R. & Mayoma Bryant	7-18-1822
Brantley, John H. & Mrs. Sarah Thomas	10-16-1822
Brown, William & Fanny Griggs	5-26-1822
Baker, John & Priscilla Stapleton	12-12-1822
Brown, William & Sarah Bryant	6-16-1822
Bullock, Mitchell & Eliza Foster	1-22-1823
Brewer, James & Catherine McCollum	2-21-1823
Bishop, Asa J. & Judith Breedlove	1-15-1824
Bullington, Reuben & Elizabeth Youngblood	1-13-1824
Bullington, Josiah & Rebecca Sanders	2-17-1824
Butts, Azariah & Mrs. Edy Jones	5-27-1824
Black, Ryel & Nancy Middlebrooks	6-30-1824
Brinkley, William & Mrs. Serena Reynolds	7-4-1824
Butts, James I. & Mrs. Elizabeth Butts	8-39-1824
Brantley, James & Eliza King	7-22-1824
Brazil, William & Creasey Tillman	11-24-1824
Bullock, Mitchell & Christian R. Lundy	11-30-1824
Brantley, Elijah & Rachel Buckner	12-9-1824
Bartlett, Samuel & Nancy Buie	9-1-1825
Bachelder, Josiah W. & Caroline M. Davis	11-8-1825
Brown, John W. & Martha T. Hunter	12-8-1825
Bass, John I. & Sarah P. Ellis	2-28-1826
Beasley, Jacob & Mrs. Sarepta Camp	11-26-1826
Bishop, Asa J. & Elizabeth W. Breedlove	1-16-1827
Blair, John & Attala Smith	8-2-1827
Boyer, William M. & Mary A. Hitchcock	11-8-1827
Bartlett, John Jr. & Elizabeth Vinson	12-18-1827

Breedlove, John H. & Nancy Echols	12-23-1827
Barnes, Joshua & Nancy Mapp	No date
Battle, Uriah & Amanda J. Askew	8-7-1828
Bonner, Thomas M. & Levina Rieves	12-1-1828
Barnes, George & Abia Lewis	12-30-1828
Brazil, Alsey & Elizabeth Welch	3-2-1829
Bonner, John & Frances M. Rives	4-13-1829
Butts, Frederick & Nancy Herin	7-23-1829
Barksdale, John & Frances M. Wilks	8-27-1829
Bass, James & Catharine Choice	9-24-1829
Barnhart, Charles & Nancy Caldwell	10-13-1829
Blount, Green W. & Elizabeth Minton	No date
Barfield, David & Eliza T. Barnes	11-3-1830
Breedlove, Benjamin & Margaret Smith	12-16-1830
Barnes, Jesse & Sarah Reynolds	No date
Branan, Kenan & Roweny Upchurch	2-10-1831
Bartlett, William & Elizabeth Barksdale	5-10-1831
Butts, William R. & Lucinda Moore	6-28-1831
Boughton, Seth N. Esq. & Margaret J. Fort	No date
Bacheldor, Littleberry & Elizabeth Foster	9-22-1831
Briant, Robert Clark & Martha Young Harper	2-29-1832
Butts, George Washington & Elizabeth S. Butts	12-20-1832
Bonner, Westley & Dovey Eubanks	3-7-1833
Brantley, Balda I. & Liza Williams	5-16-1833
Bustin, Edward & Mary Elizabeth Taylor	5-26-1833
Bishop, John & Mrs. Mary Shackleford	6-20-1833
Boyer, James B. & Mary Ann Elizabeth Doyle	7-9-1833
Blount, Isaac & Sarah Ezell	8-19-1833

Butts, Arthur I. & Georgia D. Thomas	10-10-1833
Bass, Ingram & Martha Choice	12-19-1833
Burran, Stephen & Mary Moon	12-26-1833
Babb, Brinkley & Missouri Ann Harris	11-9-1834
Bird, Robert & Martha Foster	11-29-1834
Brake, Esium & Miranda Thompson	2-16-1835
Blow, Richard & Mrs. Maria L. Howell	5-28-1835
Barnes, Lewis M. & Mary Mathis	6-21-1835
Barnes, Lewis R. & Eliza Duffey	10-1-1835
Butts, George M. & Louisa A. Lanier	2-25-1836
Battle, William R. & Caroline D. Mason	9-1-1836
Blount, Redding & Nancy Garrett	No date
Boler, Shadrack & Sarah Robertson	9-13-1836
Berry, James Edward & Georgia Anne Devereux	11-23-1836
Bozeman, John & Rebecca J. Pratt	1-31-1837
Boykin, Francis E. & Mary Frances Hudson	2-23-1837
Burch, Thomas & Mary C. Culverhouse	12-4-1837
Butts, Benjamin K. Esq. & Mary Ann T. Denton	5-30-1837
Bass, Milton & Ann Elizabeth Culver	4-20-1837
Boream (?) Benjamin F. & Jane Harwell	8-29-1837
Buckner, James & Frances Barnes	11-2-1837
Bishop, Alfred & Emily A. C. Donnelly	No date
Brantley, Elijah & Ann Brantley	1-10-1838
Butts, James I. & Saleta H. Binion	5-17-1838
Battle, Oliver L. & Martha S. Irvin	The name of omitted & 1 turned and
Brantley, Washington H. & Theresa P. Cheely	11-8-1838

Butts, Edmund & Elizabeth Graybill	No date
Brown, Alfred E. W. & Virginia Brookins	8-7-1839
Barnes, James W. & Caroline A. Greene	10-24-1839
Butts, Edmund A. & Sarah Ann Brundage	11-12-1839
Birdsong, John L. & Pamelia I Andrews	12-4-1839
Boyer, John & Saletha M. A. Veal	2-25-1840
Brundage, John Jackson & Henrietta Moore	9-27-1840
Burton, Thomas W. & Hannah W. Jackson	No date
Barrow, James & Julia Frances Belding	7-29-1841
Beecom, Campbell & Anna Twilley	7-21-1842
Barnhart, Robert & Susan B: Griggs	No date
Barnhart, John & Ann Thompson	10-11-1842
Beason, John L. & Winifred Watts	1-19-1843
Brantley, Lunsford F. & Christiline M. Waller	3-19-1843
Bell, George & Emaline E. Thomas	7-12-1843
Bullington, James M. & Caroline Denton	10-8-1843
Boyington, Montgomery & Sabrina Brown	10-19-1843
Beckham, Osborn & Elizabeth Bartlett	10-26-1843
Blanchard, Silas M. & Mary William Bass	12-3-1843
Bass, George W. & Lavinia Susan Latimer	1-4-1844
Brown, George W. & Adaline L. Kelly	3-19-1844
Brodnax, Robert B. & Catharine Waller	No date
Brown, Dr. Algernon S. & Elizabeth A. C. Rives	4-3-1844
Brown, James M. & Louisa M. Ransom	9-10-1844
Boyer, George & Ann Conner	11-4-1845
Bonnell, John M. & Cornelia F. Haynes	12-19-1845
Barnhart, Brice & Emily Ledbetter	12-21-1845
Brooks, William W. & Phoebe A. Lupo	12-30-1845

Binion, John R. & Frances L. Butts	3-4-1845
Brantley, Thomas J. & Jane Middlebrooks	2-5-1846
Brady, James & Mary B. Mitchell	8-28-1846
Brookins, Haywood & Nancy Trawick	No date
Burk, Jordan S. & Henrietta H. Hill	3-4-1847
Bloodsworth, James H. & Sarah Green	4-4-1847
Buckner, Joel & Sidney Logue	No date
Branham, Isham Richardson & Julia Maria Iverson	11-3-1847
Bass, John I. & Isabella E. Lockhart	2-15-1848
Bird, William Edgeworth & Sarah C. J. Baxter	2-24-1848
Brown, Edwin D. & Mary F. Parish	4-2-1848
Brown, William G. & Maria H. Mitchell	6-11-1848
Bryan, Col. Goode & F. Maria Myers	7-25-1848
Burnett, William H. & Frances M. Soulard	9-10-1848
Battle, John R. & Susan Pierce	10-3-1848
Battle, Dr. Henry S. & Elizabeth M. Pierce	10-3-1848
Brown, Mansel T. & Fannie D. Lewis	11-3-1848
Brown, John S. & Mrs. Elizabeth S. Thornton	1-11-1849
Burton, George W. & Sarah A. E. Harper	6-7-1849
Brake, William & Caroline Waller	7-4-1849
Brodnax, William & Martha Stevenson	7-29-1849
Berry, Fritz William & Sarah Ann Strother	11-19-1850
Chain, William L. & Sally Whatley	4-5-1810
Carter, David & Lucy Wailes	2-5-1807
Clark, Willie & Sarah Hawkins	2-19-1807
Crittendon, Robert G. & Nancy Crowder	7-13-1807
Cook, David & Lucy Miller	10-8-1807

Carson, David & Nancy Brantley	12-22-1807
Curry, William & Comfort Lary	1-17-1808
Cook, Thomas & Melbry Morriss	1-28-1808
Chambers, Robert & Jane Griggs	2-6-1808
Castleberry, Jobe & Mehaly Kelly	2-16-1808
Cator, Philip & Phthriba Wooten	3-16-1808
Culver, Warrand & Hannah Allen	10-15-1807
Carrell, Richmond & Sarah Driver	1-30-1806
Collier, Henry & Nancy Bird	3-30-1808
Culver, Augustus & Polly Wales	No date
Clower, Morgan & Silvy Laseter	1-5-1809
Cottle, William & Tabitha Self	9-3-1809
Curry, Allen & Silvy Wilson	No date
Casey, Elijah & Elsey Vinson	2-12-1810
Candler, Henry & Mrs. Elizabeth Reid	2-20-1810
Chain, William L. & Mrs. Sally Whatley	4-5-1810
carter, Girard & Rebecca Thomas	12-28-1809
Crowder, William B. & Martha Harris	No date
Cook, Nathan & Sally Atkinson	9-27-1810
Connell, Newday & Polly Simms	12-24-1809
Champion, Alexander & Polly Benson	11-22-1810
Cooper, Joseph & Susan Thomerson	11-29-1810
Collins, Benj. & Sidney Foster	9-26-1811
Culwell, William & Sally Carmeen	12-5-1811
Collins, William & Sophia Williams	12-19-1811
Culver, Isaac & Margarett Grace	11-21-1811
Culver, Nathan Jr. & Nancy Rayfield	1-9-1812

Curry, Allen & Silvey Wilson	11-30-1809
Chambers, John Esq. & Mary M. Lucas	5-7-1812
Cureton, William & Frances Brazil	7-2-1812
Cook, Isaac & Elizabeth Bonner	2-14-1811
Carmean, James & Peggy Miller	8-25-1812
Copeland, John & Eliza Rogers	9-3-1812
Cook, Allen & Lyddia Joice	9-24-1812
Collins, George & Sally Rayfield	1-21-1813
Cruse, George & Nancy Bridges	6-24-1813
Carew, Richard H. & Mary Kenon	-15-1814
Cureton, James & Phebe Patterson	8-12-1813
Clark, William & Betsey Wyley	8-8-1814
Collins, Benjamin John David & Kizia Foster	6-29-1814
Carter, Moses & Cealey Jones	1-16-1815
Connard, John & Mary Cannon	4-24-1815
Cheely, Thomas & Leah Latimer	7-13-1815
Cheely, John & Sarah Thomas	7-20-1815
Cremean, Rickets & Micha Simms	10-1-1815
Christie, Joseph & Nancy Cureton	12-21-1815
Castleberry, Elisha & Jinny Feilds	3-14-1816
Carter, Kindred & Margaret Blair	8-21-1816
Culver, Joseph & Mary Saunders	8-22-1816
Carter, Jacob & Elizabeth Averret	No date
Cooper, Beverly & Sarah Gordy	11-28-1816
Cook, Samuel & Martha Andrews	12-19-1816
Curry, James & Celeta Pruett	12-19-1816
Curry, Josiah & Polly Conner	12-29-1816
Cullins, Georgia & Sally Allen	12-26-1816

Cadenhead, James & Catherine Edge	1-2-1817
Curey, Isaac & Elizabeth Conner	No date
Curry, Isaac & Rebecca Cureton	4-6-1817
Caruthers, Thomas & Elizabeth Halley	3-30-1817
Carter, Jacob & Elizabeth Averett	11-14-1816
Cain, Isaac & Elizabeth Johnson	No date
Culver, James & Patsey Evans	5-12-1818
Collins, Robert & Sarah Ann Crawford	9-17-1818
Crilposs, James & Nancy Steward	No date
Cureton, William & Sarah H. Parker	No date
Cannon, John & Theney Andrews	No date
Curry, Neil & Elizabeth Hitchcock	7-22-1819
Cox, Chappell & Mary Mathis	12-22-1819
Culverhouse, John & Susannah Amos	12-26-1819
Carrell, William & Mary Murphey	6-6-1820
Channell, John & Respah Gilbert	No date
Culver, Obediah & Nancy Jackson	12-28-1820
Cadenhead, Ivey & Nancy Pew	2-8-1821
Carter, Jacob & Alley Albritton	2-23-1821
Culver, Levin E. & Frances Brodnax	3-27-1821
Conner, John & Elizabeth Murphy	4-11-1821
Cannon, Burwell & Mary Pruitt	No date
Christmas, Jarrett & Elizabeth Johnson	No date
Carrington, Miles H. & Rebecca Robertson	7-20-1821
Cumbo, Leroy Rean & Nancy Fulgam	8-2-1821
Carter, John & Kizziah Johnson	9-30-1821
Candler, Henry & Mrs. Elizabeth Reid	No date
Collins, Jesse & Mary Watson	2-13-1822

Cato, Capt. Butt L. & Bethiah Brewer	4-16-1822
Carr, Jesse & Lucy Butts	6-25-1822
Calhoun, James S. & Caroline Ann Simmons	12-19-1822
Cole, Isaac & Mildred Waller	12-29-1822
Colquit, John H. H. & Martha H. Eley	4-24-1823
Cheely, Lewis L. & Mary Thomas	7-24-1823
Cason, Jesse & Martha Johnson	9-18-1823
Cook, Samuel & Mary Howel	12-30-1823
Coleman, Charles & Viney Wilkins	2-25-1824
Cumming, Henry H. Esq. & Julia A. Bryan	No date
Curtis, Joseph W. & Mrs. Mary Carew	4-8-1824
Coleman, Thomas Esq. & Willey A. Coleman	6-24-1824
Carnes, Dr. Robert W. & Martha L. Jones	8-2-1824
Cogburn, William & Lucinda Harrell	8-12-1824
Crutchfield, Francis P. & Rebecca Griggs	12-16-1824
Childers, John B. & Penelope Lundy	12-23-1824
Cannon, John & Sarah Bustle	No date
Carter, Asa J. & Elizabeth Alford	2-3-1825
Crawford, Joel Esq. & Sarah L. Rhodes	No date
Coleman, Washington & Harriet W. Scott	4-19-1825
Cook, James & Nancy Averett	8-28-1825
Colbert, Richmond & Martha Champion	No date
Culver, Hardy C. & Nancy Latimer	12-1-1825
Camp, Braddock & Mary Tucker	6-22-1826
Carrington, Miles H. & Nancy Robertson	7-23-1826
Clark, James N. B. & Mahala Clark	No date
Cheser, William & Rebecca Blount	12-7-1826
Cordall, Frances & Nancy Hilsman	3-8-1827

Chiles, Nimrod S. & Irena Latimer	12-19-1827
Cook, James Elias & Elizabeth Butts	12-24-1828
Curry, Thomas J. & Matilda Moore	12-28-1828
Carter, William & Mary Davis	1-15-1829
Claxton, John P. & Nancy Champion	3-12-1829
Culver, Joshua B. & Sarah Saunders	10-11-1829
Cato, James W. & Amanda L. Rabun	12-15-1829
Champion, Eli & Mary Ann Lundy	1-17-1830
Coleman, John G. & Eliza Little	No date
Cato, William P. & Maria E. C. Rabun	12-28-1830
Camp, Braddock & Mrs. Lucretia Ivey	2-17-1831
Crawford, John L. & Martha Rachel	9-22-1831
Culver, Levin D. & Amanda Melvina Brodnax	10-27-1831
Cowles, Seth & Ann Duffey	11-26-1831
Choice, Jesse & Louisa Bass	3-22-1832
Coates, Daniel S. & Milberry Johnson	No date
Chappell, Thomas & Drusilla Cook	7-24-1832
Collins, Josiah & Frances Lancaster	1-20-1833
Childers, John B. & Martha Lundy	7-31-1833
Cocke, Jack F. & Julia Ann Binion	8-15-1833
Culver, George W. & Lucinda A. Latimer	12-5-1833
Camp, Reese & Henrietta L. Massey	12-7-1834
Calhoun, William B. & Milly Ann Driskill	2-8-1835
Culver, Gabriel & Lavinia Metcalf	4-26-1836
Chambers, Kinsey & Ann Simpson	9-29-1836
Caldwell, Joshua & Mary Jackson	12-25-1836
Cooper, George M. & Charity Reynolds	No date
Culver, Leroy C. & Martha Latimer	10-5-1837

Cook, Benjamin L. & Nancy Gilbert	10-10-1837
Channell, Thomas & Mary Ann Ledbetter	12-7-1837
Culver, Myles & Catharine Barnes	12-30-1837
Castleberry, John M. & Edna Worsham	2-10-1839
Cook, Solomon & Alcey Vinson	4-3-1839
Crawford, Robert & Charity Rachel	7-23-1839
Cook, Abner A. & Catharine Berry	1-14-1840
Caldwell, William & Celia Parker	No date
Carlisle, Brantley & Elizabeth Layfield	12-30-1840
Connel, Dr. Alva & Mrs. Maria Harford	4-11-1841
Culver, Jeptha G. & Louisa L. Latimer	12-7-1841
Carroll, Allenton & Henriett Humphrey	12-4-1841
Claiborn, Robert E. & Emily Lanier	8-3-1842
Channell, Michael & Lucinda Waller	4-18-1843
Carlisle, Brantley & Frances Ann Hall	11-10-1843
Collins, Henry M. & Lisina Barnes	12-12-1844
Carr, Thaddius & Mary Ann Bass	1-14-1845
Cureton, Richard & Hester Ann Bryant	1-16-1845
Connell, Dr. Alva & Jane R. Baxter	2-6-1845
Cooper, George W. & Elizabeth Reynolds	7-20-1845
Channell, James & Caroline Moon	12-23-1845
Clark, Richard H. & Julia A. E. Cheely	5-26-1846
Cole, Jesse & Martha Ann Arnold	7-19-1846
Cook, Abner A. & Ann E. Coleman	3-23-1847
Colbert, John G. & Martha M. Whaley	No date
Culver, William H. & Louisania P. Latimer	4-37-1848
Colbert, Thomson & Martha A. Peek	10-5-1848
Cone, John S. & Sarah A. Davis	11-4-1848

Cheely, Lewis W. & Martha Rachel	8-23-1849
Culver, Henry H. & Rebecca I. Fraley	11-30-1849
Charlton, John D. & Emily A. Taylor	5-9-1850
Cain, Elizha & Ann L. Alford	5-5-1850
Connell, Daniel & Ann Elizabeth Culver	11-13-1850
Cochran, Arthur E. & Rebecca Dickson	11-7-1850
Culver, John L. & Mary Cheely	11-12-1850
Driskell, John & Nancy Butts	12-16-1806
Denson, Calley & Elizabeth Watkins	2-19-1807
Dixon, Benjamin & Polly Taylor	2-4-1808
Dyar, James & Dorcas Williams	9-9-1808
Dennis, Isaac Jr. & Sally Whittington	3-6-1806
Daniel, Samuel & Polly Evans	11-15-1808
Douglas, George & Susannah Carlisle	No date
Dixon, Wm. & Lucinda Crawford	11-21-1809
Davis, Jonathon & Polly Waller	11-30-1809
Duncan, Isaac & Elizabeth Reeves	No date
Duckworth, Jeremiah & Bethea Britt	12-28-1810
Dickson, Thomas & Seleta Kensey	2-7-1811
Dickson, Josiah & Mary McCook	6-11-1811
Daniel, Henry & Sally Black Lucas	7-31-1811
Depree, James Thornton & Elizabeth Parks	No date
Dickson, Curry & Elizabeth Shi	12-9-1812
Dickson, Thomas & Anna McCook	2-15-1814
Dent, Nathaniel & Elizabeth Dickinson	7-16-1814
Dennis, William & Sally Thompson	8-1-1814
Dennis, John & Marguerite Dennis	12-19-1814

Drury, Samuel & Sarah Williams	12-22-1814
Duckson, John & Sarah Thompson	4-27-1815
Darden, Willis & Susan Colbert	10-26-1815
Daniel, Capt. James & Mary Turner	4-4-1816
Daniel, James & Mourning Buller	10-1-1816
Duck, Jonathon & Nancy Jones	10-25-1816
Dean, David & Martha Reynolds	1-3-1816
Driskell, Christopher & Elizabeth Brantley	12-30-1815
Dyer, Otis & Maria Lee	10-2-1817
Doney, Lowden & Nancy Jernigan	8-12-1818
Dennis, Daniel & Mary Slade	11-29-1818
Danielly, Arthur & Ja e Devereux	No date
Daniel, James L. & Eliza Butts	12-3-1818
Devereux, Samuel M. & Anna Loyd	1-10-1820
Dudley, William & Elizabeth Ewing	4-12-1820
Duckworth, John & Mary Hughes	2-28-1821
Drake, Pleasant & Louisa Blankinship	4-29-1821
Dickinson, Levi & Araminta Thomas	10-17-1822
Darden, Robert R. & Apsey B. Holland	1-2-1823
Dawkins, Garland & Phoebe Ann Barksdale	11-4-1823
Dauchy, Luther & Charlotte Lundy	1-1-1824
Dickinson, Isaac & Susan Mapp	2-2-1824
Dudley, William & Rachel Ewing	3-2-1824
Davidson, John & Mrs. Mary Metcalf	5-16-1824
Dismukes, Joseph T. & Mary E. Daniel	No date
Drummond, John S. & Arianna B. Crowder	10-20-1824
Duck, Jonathon & Rebecca Jones	11-14-1824

Drewry, John & Elizabeth Pitts	10-1-1822
Drake, Beverly & Susan Griggs	7-28-1825
Drake, Cargill & Martha Drake	8-1-1825
Duncan, James & Mrs. Nancy Lightfoot	9-18-1825
Darby, James & Mrs. Sarah Henderson	10-16-1825
Dickinson, Clark M. & Mary S. Askew	12-29-1825
Dunn, John Jr. & Martha Johnson	No date
Davis, John & Frances S. Butts	4-6-1826
Dupree, Timothy R. & Permilia O. R. Kennedy	1-19-1826
Dickson, William & Ann H. Bass	10-26-1826
Dickinson, Alpheus & Penelope Askew	2-21-1828
Downs, Dennis L. & Leunda Johnson	11-3-1828
Drake, Vinis & Delpha Drake	3-19-1829
Deas, Anthony & Mary Carlile	4-27-1829
Daves, Joel P. & Rebecca M. Vickers	12-15-1829
Dunn, Augustus B. & Rebecca Kelley	1-7-1830
Duckworth, Almon & Cyntha Giles	12-23-1830
Dunn, William & Rhoda Ransom	2-1-1831
Dunn, James K. & Malinda Kelley	5-18-1831
Dunn, John E. & Elmira Jernigan	6-19-1831
Duggan, Edmund & Elizabeth Swint	7-13-1831
Dense, Benjamin F. & Ann B. Mershon	10-21-1832
Dickinson, Joel P. & Martha D. R. Askew	1-7-1834
Dudley, Thomas & Betheny Dennis	2-16-1837
Davis, Elias & Piety Sellars	No date
Davis, George W. & Martha Hall	4-12-1838
Daniel, William & Julia Ann Sumler	7-1-1838

Dickerson, Alfred H. & Louisa M. Kelsey   2-7-1839

Dupree, Lewis G. & Mrs. Julia E. Wootan   4-30-1839

Davis, John & Betheny Rachel   6-20-1839

Dewees, William H. & Mrs. Araminta Randall   10-3-1841

Devine, John & Mary Archy   10-5-1841

Davenport, James M. & Sarah Ann Seals   11-11-1841

Davis, George W. & Caroline E. Howell   9-16-1842

Davenport, John & Ann Frances Bledsoe   3-17-1842

Dickson, William & Eliza A. Dickson   6-22-1842

Dickson, William C. & Caroline E. Palmer   1-15-1843

Devereux, Albert Crawford & Mary Ann Rebecca Bass 6-21-1843

Denton, John B. & Nancy Hester   No date

Denton, John & Elizabeth Blount   11-20-1843

Dickinson, Alpheus & Lucinda V. Austin   11-25-1845

Driskill, William B. & Elizabeth Amanda Dickson 12-3-1845

Davis, Andrew L. & Elizabeth A. Hardwick   12-9-1845

Davis, William & Mary C. Audas   1-8-1846

Dunn, John E. & Malinda A. Howell   8-30-1847

DuBose, Charles W. Esq. & Catharine A. Richards 6-20-1848

Ezell, Henry & Keziah Huskin   11-20-1806

Ernest, George & Sarah Dennis   1-22-1807

Evans, David & Frances Respess   2-11-1807

Epps, Chisholm & Polly Chapel   2-26-1807

Ellis, William & Mary Harrisson   1-26-1808

Evans, Starling & Acquilla Davidson   6-27-1809

Ewing, William & Charity Veazey   10-19-1809

Epps, Edward & Mrs. Patsy Sledge	11-31-1809
Eubanks, John & Susannah Moore	7-28-1813
Evans, Britton W. & Elizabeth K. Waller	7-18-1815
Edwards, Dr. Andrew & Blanche K. Morgan	12-26-1815
Ezell, Benjamin & Rebecca Ezel	1-16-1817
Ezell, John & Elizabeth Morris	12-29-1815
Ewing, Jonathon & Elizabeth Thompson	3-5-1818
Ennis, Charles & Elenor Moman	9-3-1818
Eubanks, Edward & Nancy Bonner	10-13-1819
Eley, James I. & Hannah Parrott	No date
Edwards, Pilot H. & Elizabeth Green	1-31-1822
Ewing, Jonathon & Nancy Turner	1-12-1823
Eubank, Richard G. & Rachel Thorpe	9-4-1823
Eubanks, Yearnest & Mrs. Mary Skinner	7-6-1824
Edwards, Jacob & Rebecca Womack	No date
Edwards, Alexander F. & Mrs. Rebecca Lucas	4-19-1825
Edge, Joshua & Penelope Pugh	12-19-1826
Ely, John W. ' Virginia A. Baugh	No date
Ellis, Green B. & Anne N. Litt	12-18-1828
Eubanks, Martin & Sarah McKinne	No date
Ellis, Joshua & Martha Murphey	10-15-1829
English, John & Lavina Wilkins	No date
Evans, John & Rachel J. Sanford	1-30-1831
Ezell, Willis W. & Nancy Gregory	8-30-1831
Ewing, Samuel Esquire & Mrs. Martha Griffis	12-24-1831
Evans, John R. & Sarah W. Battle	No date
Evans, Junus L. & Melissa Jane Morris	1-16-1833
Equals, Peter & Virginia Ann E. Berry	No date

Ellis, Levin H. & Maria Culver 3-19-1833

Ezell, Elbert L. & Frances Kelly 11-24-1836

Eubanks, Thomas & Eliza Dickson .... No date

Edwards, James I. & Lucinda S. Culver 3-1-1837

Ellis, Isaac H. & Elizabeth S. Alford 6-15-1837

Eubanks, George & Sarah Eubanks 4-28-1839

Ellis, Irwin C. & Sarah Ann Layfield 12-30-1840

Evans, Sterling G. & Mary E. West 11-14-1843

Ezell, Greenberry G. & Emaline Culver 5-26-1844

Ennis, Pleasant & Evalina Minor 1-9-1845

Evans, Joseph & Georgia Ann Peek 2-25-1847

Evans, John M. & Mary White 2-25-1849

Ezell, James Marion & Amanda Terrell Gary 11-22-1849

Figgs, James & Ann M. Greenwood 11-28-1805

Fulgham, Stephen & Nancy Taylor 12-24-1805

Fench, William & Sallie Gilbert 12-23-1806

Flournoy, Laurence & Mary Bradford 11-1-1808

Foason, Thomas & Polly Dean .... No date

Foster, John & Nancy Wright .... No date

Ferrell, Mickelberry & Martha H. D. Tyas 5-24-1810

Fort, Arthur & Eliza Jernagen 5-10-1810

Figs, James & Polly Ellis 2-21-1812

Forsyth, John & Gillah Waller 12-6-1812

Ferrell, John & Elizabeth Tyson 4-28-1814

Foard, Valentine & Hannah Cannon 6-25-1815

Ferrell, Bryan & Sarah Farr 5-29-1816

Foster, Francis & Cynthy White 12-17-1816

Franklin, Singleton & Candis Temple	2-2-1817
Fannin, James W. & Ann P. Fletcher	2-11-1817
Fears, Richard & Gatty M. Turner	9-26-1819
Fretwell, Collin A. & Elizabeth Henderson	12-9-182
Foster, Samuel & Mary A. M. Thomas	No date
Ferrell, James H. & Rebecca Brantley	No date
Flet cher, John & Nancy Farrell	3-3-1825
Fraley, William & Demaris Ingram	5-12-1825
Foster, Allen & Adaline Frazier	10-27-1825
Flowers, James M. & Phillis Waller	9-17-1827
Flournoy, Mathew H. & Eliza P. Wright	6-15-1826
Ford, William P. & Julia Ann Harris	11-2-1826
Francis, Cordall & Nancy Hilsman	3-8-1827
Fannih, James W. & Minerva D. Fort	4-24-1828
Floyd, John & Mary Ann Hunt Alston	12-3-1829
Fraser, Duncan & Evaline G. Watkins	11-25-1830
Foster, John & Mary Ann Cook	11-6-1834
Farr, Thomas & Martha Ann Hicks	7-30-1835
Ferguson, William P. & Sara Jane Burton	12-22-1835
Foster, Abner & Margaret Turner	12-6-1836
Fraley, William & Martha I. Massey	9-21-1843
Foster, Abner & Nancy E. Jackson	10-29-1843
Foster, John & Ann Barnes	4-16-1844
Foster, John & Frances Shivers	2-10-1846
Fenn, Milligan M. & Martha A. V. Nowling	6-22-1846
Farrell, James B. & Gracy Barnes	2-11-1849
Foster, N. G. & Margaret E. Vinson	7-17-1849

Frazier, Ransom B. & Elizabeth G. Pound	10-25-1849
Field, John & Sarah E. Cooper	1-34-1850
Freeney, Augustus & Naomi Rainwater	9-22-1850
Garrett, Edmond & Elizabeth Simms	4-16-1806
Greene, Burwell & Hannah Tucker	11-10-1806
Gilbert, Edmond & Amy Garrett	11-25-1806
Gillom, William & Sphiah Foard	12-8-1807
Garner, Redic & Hannah Cook	4-3-1808
Garey, Hartwell & Rebecca Stanton	5-5-
Giles, John & Mary Tarver	9-2-1808
Greer, Robert & Mary Veazey	2-27-1806
Gallman, Benjamin & Sarah Moor	6-17-1806
Griggs, William & Polly Allen	1-30-1809
Glistne, Nathaniel & Nancy Dennis	2-36-1809
Gay, Sherwood H. & Betsy Harper	No date
Goodwin, John & Lydia Speights	6-20-1809
Griggs, William & Eliza Bingham	8-20-1809
Green, Jean & Penny Pully	9-15-1807
Girard, Carter & Rebecca Thomas	12-28-1809
Greene, Coleman & Patsy Tucker	12-21-1809
Grantham, William & Edy Williams	1-1-1811
Grant, James & Nancy Sturdivant	9-23-1810
Garland, William D. & Ann H. Norris	9-10-1812
Hlazier, Westley & Sally McAlister	4-30-1813
Griggs, James & Mrs. Sally Allen	8-28-1814
Goodwin, Barnaby & Frances Pope	4-35-1814
Griggs, Lee & Agatha Sikes	7-14-1814

Greer, Gilbert & Martha Moore	9-23-1814
Griffin, Richard & Hannah Cureton	12-23-1814
Goodwyn, William W. & Jane Sanders	No date
Gary, Richard & Nancy Leath Parham	4-3-1815
Griffin, John & Charlotte Colwell	6-4-1815
Goodwin, Jefferson & Marcilla P. Williamson	6-25-1815
Graybill, John & Nancy Choice	11-7-1815
Goar, Phares & Anna Miles Culver	2-15-1816
Greene, John & Sarah Youngblood	2-29-1816
Griggs, Robert & Martha Ellington Morgan	4-11-1816
Gordy, William & Anna Griggs	11-18-1815
Goodman, Casper & Mrs. Catharine Harris	6-30-1816
Grace, Silas & Eliza Lochart	10-17-1816
Griggs, Henry & Ann Sturdivant	10-30-1816
Gordy, George & Sevene Calhoun	12-33-1816
Gordy, Thomas & Sarah Hall	1-28-1817
Goar, Faris & Anna Mills Culver	2-15-1816
Griggs, Thomas & Hannah Drake	1-1-1818
Goldsmith, John T. & Sarah Collins	No date
Griggs, Robert & Eliza M. Griggs	1-8-1818
Gupton, Athelston & Susanna Dunn	No date
Griggs, William W. & Harriet Davis	No date
Griggs, Nathaniel & Sarah Gaulding	11-3-1818
Greene, Robert & Luzancy Richardson	10-14-1819
Goodwin, Theophilus & Sustatia Thompson	11-11-1819
Gordin, Fountain & Frances Brantley	2-10-1820
Gary, James & Elizabeth Knowles	2-22-1820

Gardner, Sterling & Elizabeth Hawkins	5-23-1820
Griggs, Elkins & Lucy Drake	No date
Griggs, Henry & Elizabeth Crowder	3-29-1821
Grantham, Henry & Catharine Johnson	3-25-1821
Gladding, Jonathan & Lydia Reaves	5-8-1821
Grace, Jeptha & Martha Culver	5-13-1821
Greene, Joseph H. & Agnes Gaulding	10-16-1821
Gilliland, Lucas & Elizabeth Warren	4-10-1822
Green, John S. & Lucy Cook	10-1-1822
Gary, Alfred B. & Emily P. Sanford	2-4-1823
Gwinn, Thos. & Mary Porter	11-23-1823
Green, Wm. G. & Lucinda F. Hudson	12-18-1823
Gay, Solomon & Hannah Cureton	No date
Given, John P. & Clarissa H. McGee	8-29-1824
Gibony, Wm. & Elizabeth Ransom	12-14-1824
Gregory, John C. & Sarah H. Little	12-22-1824
Green, Phillip H. & Mildred A. W. Sanford	2-8-1825
Griggs, Henry & Lucy Brodnax	3-8-1825
Green, Daniel & Sophia Griggs	6-14-1825
Grayham, George & Deborah White	9-15-1825
Garrett, John & Sarah Long	12-11-1825
Griffis, Henry & Rebecca Cureton	1-19-1826
Gary, Henry & Laruhama Palmer	2-2-1826
Glover, Isham & Martha Johnson	2-26-1826
Gilbert, Darius & Eliza H. Hardwick	10-12-1826
Griffin, Thos. & Rebecca Holliman	12-28-1826
Grant, Charles & Elizabeth Murphy	12-29-1826

Grace, Cannon W. & Mary Ann Barnes	1-7-1827
Gilbert, Allen & Elizabeth J. Dickinson	No date
Gilbert, Thomas & Mary Bartlett	8-30-1828
Green, Thos. F. & Adeline E. A. Crowder	12-4-1828
Gardner, Elias & Martha P. Edwards	No date
Gonder, James E. & Martha A. Latimer	1-15-1829
Griggs, Green B. & Phereba D. Echols	7-23-1831
Gilbert, Nathan & Mary P. Burch	No date
Gregory, John & Martha Newman	8-22-1833
Gondor, Joseph B. & Eliza K. Taylor	11-27-1833
Gland, Joseph D. & Edith Bartlett	5-23-1835
Garrett, Jno. & Nancy Amerson	2-23-1837
Garner, Wm. & Sarah Johnson	12-31-1837
Garey, Abner & Elizabeth Thornton	1-23-1838
Green, John & Mary Jane Reynolds	1-15-1839
Gary, James & Sarah E. Harper	10-10-1839
Giles, John & Mrs. Lucy Wofford	7-28-1840
Gilmore, Hugh & Winston S. Garland	9-3-1840
Grabill, Jesse G. B. & Mary F. Dickson	1-14-1841
Greene, William T. & Caroline Clarke	No date
Goodwin, Thomas J. & Louisa L. Seals	8-4-1841
Grace, Hardy C. & Permelia Seals	12-15-1842
Gardner, Burton R. & Martha Elizabeth Scuddy	12-21-1842
Griggs, Francis J. & Elizabeth Hutchings	9-11-1842
Gladding, Wm.H. & Martha H. Pound	6-14-1843
Gardner, Nathaniel E. & Elizabeth E. Harper	1-22-1845
Garland, Robert N. & Sarah Ann Templin	6-1-1845
Gentry, Nicholas & Sarah Ann Barnes	30th - 1845

Grant, Joseph & Julia J. Parker	11-20-1845
Griggs, Wm. & Caroline Standley	No date
Gordy, George Washington & Nancy Hester	11-18-1847
Gordy, Andrew Jackson & Jane Carr	12-15-1847
Griggs, Benjamin R. & Mrs. Catharine J. Harris	3-2-1848
Garrett, Thos. J. & Eliza Twilley	4-17-1848
Grigsby, Wm. B. & Elizabeth R. Thomas	4-28-1848
Garrott, Wm. F. & Sarah L. Rachel	No date
Garrett, George F. & Elizabeth F. Jackson	1-25-1849
Horton, Elisha & Elizabeth Allen	12-11-1806
Horn, John & Elizabeth Houghton	12-31-1806
Howell, Joseph & Nancy Allen	7-16-1807
Hudgins, William & Jane Reid	7-20-1807
Hosea, Thomas & Elizabeth Cathill	9-17-1807
Herring, Arthur & Milly Barrett	11-1-1807
Huddleston, Isaac & Marah Spikes	12-20-1807
Humphrey, Thos. & Sally Howell	4-24-1808
Hollis, Richard & Milly Garrett	4-13-1806
Hutchinson, Parr & Nancy Peavy	4-6-1806
Hawkins, Robert & Elizabeth Horn	8-31-1806
Hudson, Wm. & Fanny Long	8-28-1806
Hill, Asa & Elizabeth Barksdale	10-6-1808
Haimes, Wm. & Rezpa Moore	10-25-1808
Hicks, Thos. & Elizabeth Spights	No date
Hudson, Charles & Elizabeth Reese	11-24-1808
Hutchings, Edward & Sally Logue	12-15-1808
Henry, Joseph & Polly Minton	11-24-1808

Hill, John & Libbia Morgan	No date
Hudson, Thomas & Sophia Thurmond	6-20-1809
Hutchinson, Robt. & Elizabeth Seynore	1-1-1808
Harrison, Jesse & Lydia Roe	12-21-1809
Huff, Wm. & Polly Wheeler	12-28-1809
Herindines, Silas & Polly Pound	No date
Herring, Wm. & Betsy Earp	9-30-1810
Hunter, James & Elizabeth Tucker	9-6-1810
Haynes, Thomas Jr. & Rebecca S. Lewis	10-9-1810
Horn, John & Rebecca Harry	11-9-1810
Hill, Laurence & Betsy Goodwin	3-7-1811
Henry, Daniel & Sally Black Lucas	7-31-1811
Hitchcock, John & Suckey Baker	6-16-1811
Hunter, Joseph & Penelppe Nunnery	8-6-1811
Hollomon, Eaton & Sarah Dickson	10-24-1811
Harrison, Joseph & Elizabeth Lyons	1-26-1812
Humphrey, William & Jemima Seals	1-2-1812
Horton, Wm. & Polly Harper	3-15-1811
Harrison, James & Eliza Bledsow	7-30-1812
Hudson, Irby & Jane F. Flournoy	12-22-1812
Humphrey, Robt. & Tabitha Morris	3-9-1813
Howle, Thos. T. & Nancy B. Adams	2-6-1813
Hagan, Charles & Sally Pullen	7-15-1813
Houghton, John & Ann Macon	7-8-1813
Horton, Robert & Elizabeth Saunders	7-15-1813
Hall, Thomas H. & Sally Saunders	2-1-1814
Hearne, Selby & Eliza Ransom	12-16-1813

Hargrave, Dudly & Mary Dejernett	9-27-1814
Hicks, John & Patsey Tamplin	11-10-1814
Huff, Thos. & Elizabeth Adams	No date
Holoman, Wm. & Sarah Newman	4-2-1815
Hunter, Wm. & Nancy Rives	No date
Hargrove, Daniel I. & Loodicy Brantley	12-23-1813
Hoyle, Wm. & Martha Gordy	10-25-1815
Hall, William & Sarah Sasnett	1-18-1816
Hart, James & Mary Bell	2-8-1816
Harris, Brittain D. & Jane W. Saunders	5-21-1816
Hamilton, George & Elviry Ewing	9-5-1816
Harris, John G. & Elizabeth Saunders	11-21-1816
Harris, Peterson & Rebecca Hurt	11-28-1816
Harris, Samuel H. & Nancy Smith	12-19-1816
Horton, John & Mary Allen	No date
Huckeby, Jeremiah & Elizabeth Fulsom	1-22-1817
Huff, Andrew & Margaret Rhodes	2-25-1817
Haynes, Thomas Jr. & Catharine Davis	6-15-1817
Hawkins, Drury & Sarah Walton Smith	7-16-1817
Hart, Isaac & Sally Cridette	No date
Haigood, G. Elijah & Elvy Peevy	No date
Hester, Willis & Rachel McDaniel	1-15-1818
Huff, Green & Martha Lockhart	2-12-1818
Hazel, Mathew & Mary Brewer	7-14-1818
Harrell, Wm. & Elizabeth Rachels	8-24-1818
Harden, Adam & Riscellar Adams	No date
Harris, Henry & Mary Sasnett	10-15-1818

Halcomb, Henry B. & Louisanna A. Devereux	12-17-1818
Hart, William & Nancy Bell	No date
Herrin, Peter & Mrs. Mary Griggs	1-9-1819
Hutchinson, Elijah & Sina Lee	No date
Howard, Ezra S. & Margaret Dickson	9-26-1819
Herrington, Luke & Lennah Echols	12-16-1819
Hays, George & Elizabeth Hill	1-6-1820
Holsey, Gideon & Louisa M. Grigg	2-1-1820
Hudson, Hampton & Nancy Youngblood	2-17-1820
Hall, Leonard B. & Mary D. Roberson	3-14-1820
Hammill, Wm. S. & Eliza Turner	4-18-1820
Hitchcock, David & Civil Reaves	9-6-1821
Howard, Thacker B. & Sarah G.W.Thweatt	7-24-1822
Hall, Martin Esq. & Mary McCook	12-12-1822
Hagood, Rev. Gideon & Mrs. Mary Brown	2-2-1823
Humber, Robert & Mrs. Mary E. Davis	2-12-1823
Harper, Wyatt & Ruth M. Choice	2-26-1823
Harrell, James & Sarah Ray	6-16-1823
Hyman, Aaron & Avey Melton	7-27-1823
Hollomon, Burwell & Ione Conner	8-21-1823
Hicks, Daniel & Mary Hollomon	11-15-1823
Huff, Dolaston & Rebecca E. Denson	12-11-1823
Harris, Miles Green & Caroline Hurt	1-20-1824
Harper, Capt. Benjamin I. & Mrs. Martha Trawick	4-22-1824
Holt, Pulaski S. & Lavina Richardson	No date
Hardwick, Richard S. & Martha S. Hamilton	4-19-1825
Hendrick, John & Mary Chamblain	7-22-1825

Hall, Leonard B. & Nancy Waller	9-25-1825
Holoman, John C. & Sarah L. Bridges	No date
Holland, Benjamin Esq. & Mrs. Charlotte Ingram	11-1-1825
Haynes, Doctor Wm. P. & Maria T. B. Brooking	11-30-1825
Harrill, John & Martha Hyman	1-12-1826
Hardwick, James J. & Melissa J. Pride	1-19-1826
Hall, Dixon Jr. & Elizabeth Harris	2-2-1826
Holsey, Hopkins & Elizabeth B. Mitchell	6-27-1826
Harwell, Alexander Isham & Sophronia V. Cato	8-17-1826
Hart, Samuel & Martha Veazey	10-2-1826
Hammock, Mancie & Martha Ann Amoss	11-7-1826
Hancock, John & Jane Johnson	12-18-1826
Hood, Bryant & Mary Wilkins	2-8-1827
Howard, Greenberry G. & Temperance Wilson	2-27-1827
Harris, Drury L. & Eleanor R. Barksdale	5-17-1827
Harris, James & Sara N. Andrews	7-26-1827
Hubert, Benjamin F. & Miranda H. Pride	10-10-1827
Holloman, Daniel & Rebecca Griffin	9-6-1827
Harrell, Jesse & Mrs. Catharine Miles	2-12-1828
Hillsman, James L. & Emeline Hudson	10-25-1828
Hall, David W. & Elizabeth B. Clayborne	12-11-1828
Hoyle, John H. & Harriet Saunders	1-4-1829
Holt, Robert Augustus & Emaline C. Randall	2-5-1829
Hunter, Henry & Mrs. Elizabeth Bonner	3-24-1829
Holt, Wm. & Rosena Osborn	6-23-1829
Harvill, Doctor Thomas G. & Jane Hudson	8-25-1829

Howell, Joseph & Maria L. Edwards	12-8-1829
Harper, Prestley & Eliza M. Harton	No date
Humphrey, Mathew & Charity Ewing	12-27-1829
Harrison, Alexander B. & Lucy W. Claborn	1-27-1830
Harris, Joseph C. & Martha C. Tucker	No date
Harris, James & Winney Elizabeth Lawrence	12-9-1830
Harrod, Jesse & Louisa Lewis	4-21-1831
Hutching, Boswell & Eliza Ann Garland	4-34-1831
Harford, William Hy & Maria M. Bryan	No date
Horton, Alfred M. & Rebecca Holmes	8-11-1831
Harris, Benjamin T. & Judy Ann Sasnett	10-20-1831
Hudson, Isaac & Mary Youngblood	12-22-1831
Hollomon, Terry & Lucinda Smith	1-12-1832
Hunt, James M. & Margaret Lawrence	7-31-1832
Hillsman, James & Mrs. Amanda J. Battle	7-29-1832
Hayes, John & Sarah Hill	8-15-1832
Henry, Washington & Margaret Waller	11-24-1832
Hester, David & Martha Martini	1-10-1833
Horton, Joel W. & Elizabeth Seals	9-11-1833
Harris, Absolam S. & Sarah J. Sasnett	10-31-1833
Hicks, Henry H. & Sarah Ann Williams	No date
Hamlett, James Jr. & Mary J. Lancaster	12-5-1833
Hull, Wm. T. & Murium Trawick	1-9-1834
Haynes, Chas. Eaton, & Sarah J. Ross	3-6-1834
Hutchings, Robert & Martha Ann Culver	11-23-1834
Hamill, William S. & Mrs. Mary Turner	12-31-1834
Hester, David & Mary Blount	9-26-1835
Hall, John M. & Martha B. Birdsong	11-5-1835

Hill, Abraham S. & Susan F. Holsey	11-25-1835
Hitchcock, John & Elizabeth Trawick	2-9-1836
Hancock, Thos. & Jane Pettigrew	9-22-1836
Harris, Patrick H. & Polly Bartlett	11-16-1836
Hurt, Wm. & Elizabeth R. Bass	11-4-1836
Harton, Jesse W. & Tabitha A. Smith	1-19-1837
Hutchings, Thos. L. & Mary S. Stanton	6-6-1837
Humphrey, Anderson D. & Sarah Grant	8-29-1837
Harrison, Lazarus & Lucinda Howell	9-17-1837
Hudson, Wm & Martha Ann Lawrence	1-4-1838
Humphrey, Daniel S. & Narcissa Oliphant	12-5-1838
Hudson, Col. Irby & Martha W. Walker	2-20-1840
Harris, Robert G. & Sophia Bryan	2-25-1840
Hutchings, Robert & Mrs. Martha Harper	3-24-1840
Harris, Myles G. & Eunice S. Ingraham	10-25-1840
Hanna, Edward & Obedience Harrell	12-22-1840
Humphrey, Anderson & Eliza Ann Oliphant	1-31-1841
Hunt, Wm. B. & Ann Eliza Alfriend	2-24-1842
Hillsman, Alexander & Caroline Griffin	3-13-1842
Harrison, William Henry & Sarah Ann Twilley	10-13-1842
Hood, Edwin & Elizabeth Tucker	9-23-1842
Harley, William I. & Mary L. A. Battle	1-17-1843
Holmes, Robert W. & Lavinia Rainwater	10-17-1843
Hitchcock, James M. & Ann Boyer	12-12-1843
Holmes, John W. & Emily J. Jackson	12-15-1844
Harris, James M. & Elizabeth B. Wiley	2-4-1845
Hall, Ransom S. & America Shivers	10-2-1845
Hester, James Irwin & Martha Mariah G. Belding	12-23-1845

Hitchcock, Irwin J. & Martha Stanley   1-11-1846

Hester, Alfred & Mary Ann Hyman   3-26-1846

Hunt, Judkins & Martha A. Allen   7-23-1846

Hilsman, Jeffrey E. & Ann H. Stokes   6-3-1847

Harper, John C. & Hyspatia Ann Binion   1-18-1848

Hunt, Thomas M. & Mrs. Martha Ann Lewis   5-10-1848

Hunt, Judkins & Rebecca Alfriend   7-4-1848

Hart, Rupel W. & Caroline E. Soullard   9-26-1848

Harrison, Jeptha J. & Martha Falkner   11-2-1848

Hester, William & Martha McCook   11-4-1849

Ingraham, Ira & Deborah Stebbins   4-26-1816

Ivey, Jesse & Lucrétia Turner   12-30-1819

Ingram, Moses & Charlotte Berry   6-27-1820

Iverson, Alfred Esq. & Caroline S. Holt   12-3-1822

Ingraham, John & Mrs. Elizabeth Williams   11-16-1830

Irwin, Charles M. & Harriett E. Z. Battle   11-11-1834

Ingram, Jackson J. & Angelina D. Eubanks   12-14-1837

Irby, Daniel R. & Elizabeth A. Culver   3-9-1841

Ingram, John T. & Elizabeth Frances Tamplin   1-28-1844

Jackson, Isaac &Nancy Mo--   12-9-1806

Joliff, Thomas & Keddy Wallance   12-22-1807

Jackson, James & Susan Edwards   7-29-1806

Jones, Henry & Nancy Stewart   10-27-1808

Jolliff, Davis & Penny Capehart   11-10-1808

Jeter, Edmond & Lucy A. Puckett   12-7-1808

Jones, John & Mary Montgomery   12-22-1808

Jean, Green & Penny Pully	10-15-1807
Johnston, Jacob & Mrs. Nancy Biggam	No date
Johnson, Martin & Elizabeth Peace	2-22-1810
Jones, Sterling & Patsey Seales	5-30-1811
Jenkins, Robert & Patia Sanders	- - 1811
Jackson, Burwell & Maria Chapman	1-16-1812
Jenkins, Charles & Burchett Loyd	1-21-1812
Jordan, John & Priscilla Johnson	1-7-1813
Jones, Ambrose & Shady Ann Wright	3-2-1813
Johnson, Robert & Elizabeth Peek	3-8-1814
Johnson, Frederick & Mary Harris	8-2-1815
Johnson, Jacob & Vicey Fulsom	No date
Jackson, Thomas & Rachel Culver	11-18-1815
Jordan, James & Catharine Mays	7-16-1816
Justice, Isaac & Mary Youngblood	7-18-1816
Jordan, Benjamin & Patients Ingram	10-11-1816
Johnson, Ashfield & Martha Ann Lewis	No date
Johnson, Timothy & Judith Noles	7-27-1817
Johnson, Henry S. & Louiza Smith	No date
Jones, James & Sarah Carter	3-29-1818
Johnson, Evans & Mary Camp	5-21-1818
Johnson, Stephen & Mrs. Frances Pickard	7-9-1818
Jones, James D. & Ann J. Simms	11-12-1818
Jordan, Wm. & Winifred Howell	No date
Jones, Aley & Matilda Hinson	No date
Jones, John W. & Sarah H. Harris	11-24-1818
Johnson, Luke & Lucy Taylor	6-3-1819

Jones, Wm. & Martha Barksdale	No date
Judkins, Zachariah & Martha Faison	8-3-1820
Jackson, Lucas & Sarah Harrison	2-10-1822
Johnson, Isaac & Penelope Blount	3-12-1823
Jones, John M. & Margarett Eliza Thompson	10-29-1823
John, William Greene & Nicey Ettiol	12-27-1823
Johnson, Seaborn & Ann Castleberry	1-18-1824
Jones, Cullen & Levina Rosser	1-15-1824
Jones, Benjamin & Elizabeth Champion	3-10-1825
Jones, Samuel F. & Selete Jones	7-24-1825
Jones, Ezra B. & Frances M. Crowder	11-3-1825
Johnson, James & Mrs. Sarah Johnson	1-4-1826
Johnson, Stephen & Emily Higdon	2-22-1826
Jackson, Wm. & Nancy Swinney	3-23-1816
Jones, William E. & Caroline M. Randle	12-13-1827
Jones, Phillip & Nancy Ransom	12-19-1927
Johnson, Joseph & Susan Warren	1-17-1828
Johnson, Martin & Margaret Dickson	9-13-1829
Johnson, James & Bethena Johnson	5-29-1828
Johnson, Amos & Edna Ann Robertson	12-18-1828
Jackson, William & Eliza Barnes	6-4-1829
Johnson, Willie & Rachel Pruitt	12-24-1829
Jones, Anthony & Mrs. Hannah Long	No date
Johnston, Wm. & Lurana Smith	2-25-1830
Jones, James & Martha Barnes	7-13-1830
Johnson, Lewis & Mary Ann Porter	2-25-1833
Jackson, Burwell W. & Clara Harris	No date

Jenkins, Thomas J. & Nancy Carlisle	No date
Johnston, Benjamin & Penelope Osborne	12-29-1833
Jackson, Archibald M. & Angelina Perry Evans	6-19-1834
Johnson, Willis & Mary Swint	10-23-1834
Johnson, Isaac & Mary Channel	No date
Justice, John & Mary Ann Cowle	12-15-1836
Jones, Manam & Emily M. Long	2-23-1837
Jackson, Wm. S. & Martha D. Butts	6-6-1837
Jordan, Elbert & Sarah Murphey	No date
Jordan, Lucius & Sarah Jones	No date
Jenkins, Levi & Mary Ann Arnold	No date
Johnson, Seaborn & Rebecca Rowe	No date
Jones, Thomas & Eliza P. Tucker	11-12-1839
Jordan, Thomas W. & Emily Dickson	12-25-1839
Johnson, Amos & Emily Caldwell	5-25-1841
Jackson, Enoch & Mary Jane Lawson	2-17-1842
Johnston, William & Julia Johnston	12-26-1843
Johnstone, Rev. Malcolm & Sarah G. Bonner	8-3-1843
Johnstone, Richard M. & Mary Frances Mansfield	11-26-1844
Jackson, John A. & Mary Lupo	12-22-1844
Johnson, Daniel I. & Malinda Johnson	1-5-1845
Jones, John & Martha Mitchell	3-18-1845
Jenkins, Rolin & Malinda Hannah Arnold	1-4-1846
Johnson, James M. & Willie Ann Garland	No date
Jackson, Vincent W. & Martha Ann Reynolds	2-1-1849
Jarrel, Redding & Susan A. B. Dunn	8-12-1849
Jarrel, Elisha P. & Mary S. Simmons	9-9-1849

Jenkins, Mansfield & Arianna Arnold	No date
Johnson, James E. & Frances C. Watkins	10-29-1849
Jackson, Joshua B. & Mary Ann Alford	12-20-1849
Johnson, Irvin H. & Nancy Cook	9-8-1850
Jackson, Wm. H. & Sarah J. McWhorter	11-7-1850
King, Elisha & Kesiah Sanders	4-27-1809
Kilgore, Ralph & Elizabeth Clements	10-12-1810
Kelly, John & Peggie Bullock	4-21-1812
Kinnon, Thomas & Lucy Brooking	12-10-1812
Kelly, John & Frances Buckner	3-26-1815
Kendrick, Harvey & Maria G. Hall	7-5-1815
Kenerly, Everton & Elizabeth Hayes	8-3-1815
Kean, Alexander & Clarissa Smith	10-12-1817
Kindall, David & Nancy Brewer	7-29-1819
Kirkpatrick, James & Lamira Lancaster	4-4-1820
Kilgore, Benajah & Polly Skinner	2-10-1825
Knox, William B. & Hetty Wilkins	12-8-1825
King, Alfred P. & Catharine F. Lucas	12-19-1826
Kennedy, William & Nancy Foster	1-18-1827
Kirkpatrick, Elijah & Louisa Arnold	No date
Kenan, Augustus Holmes & Henrietta Green Alston	6-19-1828
Knight, Robert & Sarah Tarver	12-2-1830
Kimbrough, John & Fetna Cato	2-23-1832
King, Cyrus C. & Minerve Cordelia Palmer	1-21-1833
Knowles, Chas. R. & Mary A. Berry	12-11-1834
Kirk-Patrick, Samuel & Frances Arnold	12-23-1834

Kennedy, Seth & Maria A. Davenport	8-10-1837
Kelley, John A. & Martha Long	1-3-1838
Kelley, Elbert G. & Catharine Culver	8-8-1839
Knowles, James Madison & Laura Foster	9-19-1839
Kelley, Abner M. & Sarah Long, formerly	
Mrs. Sarah Shivers	1-24-1841
King, Brady R. & Martha Carr	1-2-1845
Knowles, Charles R. & Mary E. B. Coleman	12-18-1845
Knowles, Birdsong & Elizabeth Jane Herringdine	10-15-1846
Kitchens, Terrell & Arianna Edna Chiles	12-6-1846
Kennedy, James A. R. & Elmira A. Arnold	9-24-1849
Lewis, Asa & Nancy Thom--	No date
Lawson, David & Leathy Rees	4-10-1806
Leonard, Benjamin & Elizabeth Ouston	6-15-1806
Lovett, Samuel & Nancy Peace	No date
Lench, Gerard & Sarah Thomas	5-15-1807
Loyd, Joseph & Rachel Nelson	1-7-1808
Langford, John & Eliza Tyus	1-21-1808
Lewis, Joseph & Sally Barnes	9-27-1808
Lisle, Jesse & Fanny Reed	10-7-1805
Lewis, Augustin & Louiza Brooking	7-13-1809
Long, John & Milly White	No date
Lucas, John & Rebecca Lucas	11-25-1807
Long, Richard & Polly Brown	No date
Lawson, Dudley & Nancy Harton	No date
Layfield, John & Sally Waller	2-4-1810
Lynch, Grey & Nancy Thomas	No date

Larey, John & Betsey Pullen	No date
Levington, Thomas & Nancy Allen	9-19-1809
Logue, James & Frances Hunter	7-16-1811
Lunday, Thomas & Lurana Atkison	1-14-1812
Linch, Jaqueline & Sophia Ray	1-16-1812
Latimer, Henry W. & Lurana Smith	12-26-1811
Langford, Edmund & Joysey Willingham	2-27-1812
Lawson, Francis & Dolly Kelley	3-12-1812
Loyd, Richard & Polly Strickland	1-27-1811
Long, Crawford & Nancy Patterson	12-24-1812
Langford, Nicholas & Oncy R. Palmore	8-12-1813
Langford, Jarvis & Elizabeth Fields	1-27-1813
Latimer, John & Elizabeth Roper	2-24-1814
Lucas, William D. & Mary Dick	2-9-1814
Leavesly, Thômas & Trinity Mc Kinne	6-26-1814
Langford, George N. & Lucy M. Tyus	12-17-1816
Lamb, Greene E. & Sarah Griffin	1-16-1817
Lumsden, John G. & Melindy Sanford	11-24-1816
Lewis, Hamlin & Anna Lewis	4-26-1817
Langford, Robert & Sarah Willingham	7-10-1817
Long, Alfred & Hannah Barksdale	No date
Lawrence, Abraham & Elizabeth D. Boren	No date
Lovett, James & Martha Logue	6-18-1818
Law, Wm. & Lucy Barksdale	No date
Lucas, Wm. & Aley Rogers	8-22-1820
Lewis, Wm. & Katharine Townsend	9-19-1820
Lowe, Wm. & Elizabeth B. Rabun	No date

Latimer, Joel & Mary Latimer	No date
Lane, Henry C. & Mary Gindratt	9-20-1820
Lewis, Doctor Richard & Mary Womack	6-7-1821
Latimer, Benjamin & Elizabeth Latimer	3-8-1815
Ledbetter, James W. & Polly Carter	9-1-1813
Leek, John & Peggy Young	No date
Lucas, William & Rebecca Sanders	No date
Linch, Charles & Eliza Griggs	8-27-1816
Lucas, Walter & Mrs. Eliza H. Butts	7-30-1818
Lester, Eli & Winifred Hill	No date
Lupean, Moreland & Mrs. Mary Peek	3-9-1819
Lightfoot, James S. & Anna Lancaster	2-8-1820
Lewis, Lack & Elizabeth Wilkinson	10-25-1821
Lewis, John H. & Unity Franklin	4-25-1822
Luas, Beverly G. G. A. & Susan Lucas	6-13-1822
Lewis, William & Netty Manning	8-4-1822
Landrith, Thomas & Jane Turner	11-15-1823
Lundy, Henry & Mary Childers	4-22-1824
Leonard, Joseph & Mary Lewis	5-12-1824
Lancaster, Luertis C. & Sarah C. Everitt	6-6-1824
Lewis, Ulyssis & Sarah Ann Abercrombie	10-7-1824
Lanier, Nicholas Esq. & Nancy Sanders	5-25-1826
Lawson, Thomas B. & Mrs. Nancy Lawson	1-4-1827
Lucas, Edwin L. & Caroline E. Brooking	6-13-1827
Lundy, Williamson & Sarah D. Alford	10-2-1827
Laughlin, John O. & Sarah McWhirter	12-30-1827
Lanier, Henry M. & Olivia Smith	2-28-1828

Lewis, Major George D. & Sophia Thomas	2-26-1829
Latimer, John B. & Louisiana M. Gonder	3-19-1829
Long, Davis & Elizabeth Pickard	5-14-1829
Lewis, James G. Esq. & Martha Ann Lewis	10-29-1829
Latimer, James W. & Sarah M. Garrett	9-14-1830
Latimer, William & Tabitha Willson	9-1-1830
Lary, Dr. Samuel & Mrs. Sophia Lewis	1-20-1831
Lewis, John Wm. & Mary Ann Matilda Youngblood	2-7-1831
Lawrence, Michael & Mrs. Sally Stowers	6-30-1831
Lewis, James Madison & Emaline Henry	No date
Lamb, Green E. & Elizabeth Huckaba	2-2-1832
Lilly, David & Margaret Reed	2-9-1832
Lundy, Phillip H. & Mary Eaton Haynes	6-10-1832
Layfield, Londy & Louisa Kenady	7-22-1832
Lancaster, Thomas A. & Harriett I. Franklin	11-6-1832
Lary, James & Nelly McWhorter	1-29-1833
Little, Thomas I. & Sarah B. Lundy	7-10-1834
Loriner, James T. H. & Julia F. Skinner	12-4-1834
Larey, Daniel & Sara Ann Rebecca Thomas	6-4-1835
Lovitt, James & Nancy Rachel	No date
Loring, David & Angelina Cureton	11-26-1835
Lumbley, Henry & Falby Rachel	No date
Lester, William W. & Sarah Ann Arnold	12-8-1836
Lanier, Edward A. & Mrs. Ruthy Warren	1-5-1837
Lester, Benjamin L. & Henrietta P. Lester	3-10-1837
Loyd, James C. & Amanda C. Spillers	5-25-1837
Leonard, Coleman & Eliza J. Ledbetter	9-20-1837

Lumley, William & Sarah Mc Cook	10-24-1837
Lawson, Roger & Harriett Hitchcock	12-6-1837
Logue, Thomas & Sarah E. Melton	12-19-1837
Loring, David & Lamentation Brazille	1-25-1838
Latimer, James S. & Lilieory Shivers	10-30-1838
Lary, James & Mary Herringdine	12-30-1838
Lundy, Robert & Sinthy Barnheart	9-12-1839
Lanier, Nicholas & Mary Ann Layfield	11-23-1840
Latimer, Thomas H. & Elizabeth A. Gonder	12-15-1840
Little, John H. & Frances E. Mitchell	12-17-1840
Little, James & Sarah E. Garrett	1-14-1841
Ledbetter, James Henry & Sarah Minerva Alford	2-18-1841
Long, Wilson & Sarah Gatlin	2-28-1841
Loyd, Alston & Mrs. Frances Reynolds	3-28-1841
Lary, Henry & Narcissa Jordan	6-3-1841
Latimer, Joel & Martha Alford	8-19-1841
Long, Henry & Drusilla McWhorter	1-12-1842
Latimer, Marshall Edward & Amelia Nash Shivers	9-8-1842
Little, Littleton Ludlow & Caroline Eliza Gregory	10-27-1842
Long, Littleberry & Charity Rachel	1-25-1843
Lawrence, Michael J. & Martha Graybill	12-21-1843
Logue, James Jr. & Elizabeth Ausburn	3-2-1844
Layfield, William & Lovie Parish	1-12-1845
Lowry, Isaac H. & Julia Hudson	12-30-1845
Lane, Andrew Jackson & Frances Ann Brooking	1-16-1845
Logue, William & Emily Simmerson	No date
Logue, Thomas & Martha Ann Blount	8-11-1846
Lewis, David W. Esq. & Martha E. Meriweather	3-18-1847

Layfield, John & Georgia Ann Carlisle	1-9-1848
Lary, William G. & Mary Beckham	11-9-1848
Little, Thomas I. & Jane Maria Ware	11-1-1849
Lovett, David & Roena Johnson	1-11-1850
Logue, Joseph & Martha Dennis	9-3-1850
Latimer, Anderson J. & Catharine E. Lundy	11-28-1850
Miller, William & Phillis Ellis.	10-9-1806
Merritt, William & Nancy Norrington	10-31-1806
Maddux, John & Sally Betts	12-30-1806
Mapp, Burwell & Patsy Huckaby	6-30-1807
McGinty, Robert & Penelope Moore	7-5-1807
Moreland, Robert & Marah Porch	11-23-1807
Matthews, Charles & Polly Garey	12-22-1807
Maghee, Josiah & Nancy Davis	12-29-1807
McAlester, James & Amy Thornton	4-15-1806
Maddox, John & Polly Bradford	4-3-1806
Mattony, John & Eliza Shackleford	1-14-1808
McGee, Joseph & Matilda Brantley	12-12-1808
Mathers, Thos. & Mary Ship	4-6-1809
Mills, William & Nancy Rosser	11-21-1809
Mc Arthy, William & Sarah Tait	No date
Morris, Michael & Polly Andrews	1-3-1810
McGee, Benj. & Patsey Gay	1-9-1810
Mathis, Elisha & Nancy Mathis	2-6-1810
McLendon, Wiley & Nancy Motley	No date
Maclellan, William & Polly Bird	7-5-1810
Meggs, William & Seleta Askew	8-19-1810

McGinnty, Washington & Nancy Thompson	No date
Miller, Jonathon & Nancy Weldon	11-20-1810
McLellan, John & Clary Lee	No date
Meggs, William & Salety Askew	8-19-1810
Moore, Isaac & Unity Brown	No date
McCollin, Patrick & Betsy McCook	12-24-1811
Morris, Nathan & Sally Moss	12-6-1810
Miller, Jacob & Mary Turner	6-9-1812
McBay, Aleck & Polly Butler	9-30-1813
Martin, Gabriel & Rebecca Turner	6-5-1813
McCray, Epaphoroditus & Mary Foson	2-3-1814
Murden, Jeremiah & Mildred Lucas	2-14-1814
Mayo, Valentine & Winifred Wilder	12-19-1813
Marchman, Wryley & Patsey Powell	5-5-1814
Morgan, Wilton & Mary Carr	6-23-1814
Mathews, Robert & Julia Gary	12-22-1814
Morris, Taylor & Abigail Northern	No date
Medlock, Charles & Martha Latimer	2-9-1815
Maddox, Benjamin & Catherine Powell	2-14-1815
Mosley, Stephen & Nancy Boran	No date
Maddox, John & Polly Worsham	6-20-1815
Mapp, Robt.H. & Martha Barnes	9-25-1815
McDaniel, Daniel & Nellie Carter	8-24-1815
McDonald, George & Frankie Boman	2-25-1816
McAlister, Sanders & Martha Ferrell	6-25-1816
Moon, James & Eliner McColvin	7-11-1816
Mitchell, Maj. Robt. & Elizabeth Davis	6-13-1816

McGibony, James C. & Mary L. Adams	11-21-1816
Moon, Thos. & Penney Horton	11-28-1816
Medford, William & Rebecca Kilgore	No date
Minter, John & Dorothy Mathis	2-6-1817
Miller, Wm. & Elizabeth Conner	2-23-1817
Moore, Mark E. & Martha Dubose	3-13-1817
Miller, Solomon & Nancy Latimer	No date
Macklin, Edmund & Ann Greene	12-12-1816
Murphy, Daniel & Elizabeth Garrett	No date
Mattocks, Hamlin D. & Holley Pearce	5-4-1817
Mitchell, Julius C. B. & Catharine Daniell	No date
Mahon, William & Nancy Ross	6-9-1817
Mc Cowen, William D. & Ann Parker	12-23-1815
Mitchell, Henry & Elizabeth Whitehurst	11-27-1817
Mapp, James & Clary Wooten	10-30-1817
McDonald, Isaac & Elizabeth Morpos	4-16-1818
Mason, Thos. & Reancy Andrews	7-24-1818
Mahone, John R. & Elizabeth Gindratt	9-17-1818
Moon, James & Mary McCollum	No date
Middlebrooks, Alford & Sarah Ellis	6-30-1819
Mews, Daniel & Betsey Waller	8-5-1819
McLemore, Jones & Mary Sanders	9-15-1819
Miller, James A. & Ann G. Wallace	6-29-1820
Morgan, Simon S. & Lovey B. Cannon	8-4-1820
Mershon, Wm. & Frances Tucker	9-10-1820
Minton, Mills & Martha Brazil	9-27-1820

Mitchell, John H. & Elizabeth Mershon	11-1-1820
Moore, Elijah & Mehala Gordy	4-29-1821
Martin, Joseph & Mrs. Lucrecy Minton	6-30-1822
Morris, Thomas & Sarah Youngblood	8-25-1822
Moye, Thomas & Nancy McWhirter	11-1-1822
McWhirter, Samuel & Naomi Liggett	12-19-1822
Munsel, Seth R. & Ophelia Holt	2-14-1823
Mixon, Elijah & Charlotte Aubry	9-4-1823
Mann, Jeremiah D. & Mary Jernigan	10-14-1823
Melson, Appleton W. & Penelope Simms	1-27-1824
Mullins, Henry & Mary Butts	2-15-1824
Mallet, Samuel & Sarah Blount	8-5-1824
McCulloch, Asa & Eliza Wade	No date
Meredith, John & Rebeccah Archer	12-31-1824
Morgan, Thomas B. & Eliza G. Mitchell	9-13-1825
McKinne, Barna & Elizabeth Ferrell	5-23-1826
Mershon, William & Elizabeth Brown	12-6-1826
Miller, Raileigh & Penelope Bryant	1-1-1827
Mason, John M. & Leacy R. Andrews	No date
Miles, John J. S. & Jane M. Ewing	10-4-1827
Miller, Jacob W. & Frances D. Garland	10-25-1827
Morgan, Thomas B. & Elizar M. B. Chivers	12-12-1827
Mann, Wm. B. & Lucy Broadnax	1-1-1828
Mansfield, Eli & Nancy B. Hardwick	3-20-1828
McWhirter, Eli & Anna Reaves	3-27-1828
McCook, Daniel & Luvaney Rachels	5-8-1828

McGee, Joseph & Blanche Dunovan	1-15-1829
McCulloh, Joseph P. & Elizabeth R. Daniel	3-17-1829
Marshall, George T. Esq. & Mary E. Scott	10-22-1829
McDaniel, George M. & Ursula Robertson	No date
McLeod, Duncan & Ursula Robertson	11-19-1829
McDaniel, Wiley & Salethe Johnston	3-23-1830
McMillan, Daniel & Elmira Dansforth	No date
McDaniel, Ahiel & Jane McDaniel	10-28-1830
Moss, Gabriel Jr. & Frances B. Lundy	1-27-1831
McDaniel, Lee L. & Ann Gladin	7-31-1831
Moore, Green & Eliza L. Cook	8-25-1831
Marchman, Thos. J. & Martha L. Moon	11-24-1831
McKinnon, Hugh & Nancy Long	12-23-1832
McLeod, Daniel & Lucinda Garrett	12-30-1832
Middlebrooks, James H. & Cassandra W. Howell	2-6-1833
McMullen, Daniel & Mary Burton	4-11-1833
Marshall, Joseph & Nancy Layfield	8-19-1832
McGinty, Wm. A. & Lucretia Arnold	8-1-1833
Mercer, Dennis & Elizabeth Vinson	1-14-1834
Metcalf, Eliphalet H. & Mary J. Bonner	3-26-1834
Miller, Jonathon G. & Eliza Veal	4-17-1834
Martin, Carlisle P.B. & Margaret F. Little	6-12-1834
McCook, Wm. & Frances Hester	4-25-1834
McCook, John M. & Malinda Mc Daniel	5-1-1834
Mallory, James D. & Rincy Bachelder	11-23-1834
McCall, Jacob & Patience Rebecca Hamilton	7-2-1835
Mason, William T. & Rebecca A. Brookings	1-18-1838

Medlock, Major Montgomery S. & Henrietta S. Latimer 2-22-1838

Mason, Col. Thomas & Arianna E. Waller   5-17-1838

Mapp, Robert H. & Sarah Ann Lawson   7-19-1838

Medlock, Benjamin F. & Eliza Jane Whaley   9-13-1838

McGinty, George W. & Lavitus Rowe   11-1-1838

Martin, John T. & Ellen M. J. Navy   1-24-1839

McDaniel, Charles & Eliza Lewis   2-3-1839

Moon, Richard H. & Mary Channell   8-29-1839

Manning, Amos R. Esq. & Martha E. Lewis   4-7-1841

Moon, James W. & Mary Drake   12-28-1841

McGinty, John & Mary L. Brown   8-9-1842

Marchman, William & Priscilla Moon   No Date

Mercer, Dr. Leonidas Bennington & Mary Ann Hillsman 9-20-1842

Minton, William Rabun & Susan Lavernia Kelly   3-16-1843

Murry, Orick J. & Caroline F. Amos   6-22-1843

Mosely, Thomas B. & Va. D. Crowder   9-21-1843

McGilvary, John Esq. & Mrs. Louisa Choice   3-15-1844

McComb, Robert A. & Mrs. Mary Jane Jackson   7-30-1844

Mapp, Wm. L. & Rebecca A, Mapp   12-12-1844

McCray, Robert & Martha L. Worthy   12-31-1844

Miller, Russell Esq. & Mrs. Bertha E. Trawick   1-2-1845

Mathews, Jesse M. & Mary F. Humphrey   12-21-1845

Marchman, Risden & Eliza Moon   1-1-1846

McCray, James & Missouri Garrett   5-19-1846

McCray, Robert & Martha Ann Brantley   7-16-1846

McDaniel, Wiley & Theny Davis   1-20-1847

Martin, Archibald & Mary E. Roberts   11-16-1847

Moye, James & Martha S. Minton	12-1-1847
Minor, Francis & Mary Jane Watson	1-13-1848
Martin, Samuel & Eliza Roberts	10-17-1848
McCoy, Daniel Newton & Dicey Archer	10-24-1848
Miller, Jonathon D. & Mrs. Martha Radney	No date
McCoy, Robert J. & Sarah Archer	1-1-1849
Myers, Benjamin B. & Julia A. Underwood	5-8-1849
Miller, Jonathon/& Martha A. Crooms	No date
McDaniel, Robert & Martha Cook	9-23-1849
McCook, John & Rebecca Long	12-24-1849
Marchman, Risdon & Mary Waller	1-1-1850
Meeks, Bennet B. & Elizabeth Ann Martin	12-12-1850
Mason, Wm. J. & Mary D. Pitt	1-4-1851
Newsome, Isaac & Polly Lowe	1-15-1807
Newsome, John & Patsy Alford	2-7-1807
Noles, James & Nancy Marchman	2-12-1807
Nelson, Alexander & Cartes Sherley	4-7-1808
Nelson, Jonathan & Sarah Pimentor	1-17-1806
Newsome, Batts & Susannah Tait	No date
Norwood, John & Nancy Kelley	1-4-1811
Noles, Joseph & Levina Evans	2-27-1812
Needham, Elijah & Jinny Spinks	8-4-1812
Newsome, Wm. & Nancy Miller	10-18-1814
Newberry, James & Sophronia Pleasants	1-19-1815
Nisbet, John & Harriett Cooper	4-25-1815
Newsom, Joel D. Esq. & Martha M. Waller	7-25-1816
Nelson, George W. & Elizabeth Newsome	12-31-1816

Norwood, Thomas & Maria Barnes	No date
Nellums, Clevus A. _ Ann Howell	2-17-1824
Neil, Thomas & Martha R. Moss	No date
Newman, Richard & Mary Pervice	10-10-1824
Neel, Thomas & Anne Veazey	11-18-1828
Nelson, John K. & Martha Finn	1-26-1830
Newsom, Joel D. Esq. & Mary E. Middlebrooks	11-6-1833
Norris, Charles H. & Julia Ann Wallace	9-3-1836
Nichols, William & Charity Snyder	3-22-1838
Newsom, Joel & Elizabeth Figgs	9-27-1839
Norr, John K. & Caroline E. H. Lanier	11-24-1841
Nicholson, Alexander L. & Martha Jean	2-14-1844
Nolan, John & Sarah Gordy	10-11-1845
Neel, Thomas C. & Willie E. Latimer	12-20-1848
Nolan, Joseph & Lucinda Quinn	12-28-1848
Nelums, James H. & Minerva Hilsman	12-26-1849
Oliver, Terry & Nancy Tait	11-15-1809
Ogletree, Richard & Dolly Huff	No date
Ogletree, Richard & Mahitable Smith	No date
Orear, William & Margarette Mc Collum	No date
Owens, William & Phalba Moon	1-12-1832
Osborn, John W. & Martha McDaniel	6-19-1832
Osborn, James & Catharine McDaniel	12-16-1838
Oliphant, Solomon R. & Amanda Rainwater	3-12-1846
Osborn, James & Gracy Ann Elizabeth Wood	3-30-1848

Perry, Brittain & Polly Denny	11-25-1806
Pruitt, Lemuel & Jane R. Sutton	12-18-1806
Perkins, Uriah & Caty Montgomery	5-26-1807
Passmore, Alexander & Patsey Sikes	6-3-1807
Porch, Thomas & Betsey Reese	12-24-1807
Pritchett, Joseph & Sally Griggs	4-30-1806
Perce, Felan & Elizabeth Veal	7-19-1806
Pope, Jesse & Leah Latimer	9-32-1808
Pope, Thomas & Elizabeth Loften	11-20-1808
Pleasants, Thos & Mary Durham	No date
Porter, Robert & Elizabeth Brown	No date
Powers, John & Micca Hardwick	No date
Patterson, Joseph & Betsey Long	7-30-1809
Peavy, Charles & Rebecca Mathews	No date
Parish, Harris & Polly Spivey	12-14-1809
Purify, John & Nancy Williams	12-31-1809
Pierce, Dixon & Elizabeth Brown	No date
Pickard, Jesse & Fanny Sykes	12-28-1809
Phillips, Martin & Milly West	4-30-1809
Parker, Stephen & Betsey Smith	1-18-1810
Pound, Joel & Nelvy Blount	No date
Prewett, Elisha & Anna Huckerba	No date
Prewett, Reubin & Nancy Griffin	No date
Pouh, Thomas & Tabitha Bonner	4-17-1810
Pedigrew, Robert & Abegail Brooks	1-5-1809
Porch, Harwell & Polly Wooten	1-31-1811

Paris, Philander O. & Theney Williams	10-27-1812
Pace, Hardy & Fanny Hopkins	4-2-1812
Pearce, Thomas & Betsey Roberts	7-21-1812
Peace, Major & Bridget Gilleland	3-8-1814
Patillo, George H. & Dicey Ewing	9-1-1814
Peacock, William & Martha Patterson	11-17-1814
Peevy, Eli & Mary Youngblood	1-19-1815
Price, Wm. H. & Margaret McClelen	1-2-1815
Purkins, Alexander & Seleta Jernigan	12-26-1816
Price, Thomas & Elizabeth McClallin	1-21-1817
Palmore, Russell & Mary Spier	No date
Parish, Moses & Phereby Carr	6-29-1817
Patterson, William & Nancy Noles	7-30-1817
Potter, John & Susanna Harwell	5-5-1818
Prewett, Henry & Elizabeth Castleberry	No date
Parker, George & Betsey Mason	10-24-1817
Pettigrew, Robert & Patsey Thornton	3-4-1818
Perry, Thomas & Smith Tarver	5-2-1818
Peevey, Daniel & Elizabeth Peevey	7-27-1818
Powell, James & Mary Mershon	8-16-1818
Plunkett, Silas & Sarah Gilbert	11-24-1818
Parrish, Green & Rebecca Cadenhead	12-10-1818
Peace, Moreland Lee & Mrs. Mary Peek	3-9-1819
Parker, John & Nancy Folsome	9-7-1819
Parker, Lewis & Julia Jernigan	9-21-1819
Pressley, John & Phereby Childs	10-7-1819
Perryman, David & Ann Henderson	5-12-1820

Peace, John Jr. & Catharine Bartlett	1-10-1821
Pressley, Moses & Mrs. Elizabeth Cawthon	4-25-1821
Pruett, Joseph & Elizabeth Cannon	No date
Porch, Hartwell & Polly Wooten	1-31-1811
Pilsworth, Garrett W. & Elizabeth Wood	No date
Peace, Major & Sally Vinson	6-5-1823
Parker, Asa H. & Martha A. Foster	11-30-1823
Perry, Obediah & Eleanor H. Horton	12-11-1823
Pilcher, James & Eliza Griffin	5-13-1824
Parmer, Thomas & Frances Shearman	5-27-1824
Patterson, Solomon & Rebecca Murphey	7-27-1824
Pearce, Jesse & Mrs. Keturah Miller	No date
Pike, William T. & Elizabeth Brown	1-30-1826
Parker, Asa H. & Lucy F. Breedlove	No date
Parker, Milo B. & Missouri Thomas	11-15-1824
Pullin, Henry & Sealey Cason	8-11-1829
Peek, Osborn R. & Mary Ann Ashley	9-20-1829
Parmer, James & Mrs. Julia B. Mathis	1-5-1830
Pugh, William & Mary Ann Forsyth	6-6-1830
Pardee, Samuel A. & Emily A. B. Andrews	12-23-1830
Parish, Allen & Mrs. Amanda Reynolds	3-8-1831
Parker, Joseph & Lucy Potter Lindsay	12-16-1831
Pinkston, Green B. & Mary Sherman	9-13-1832
Pounds, James & Nancy Pickard	1-17-1832
Peek, Henry & Emily Ashley	10-12-1832
Pittit, John W. & Eliza W. Wiley	No date
Pugh, Thomas & Martha Arnold	6-23-1833

Perkins, Adams N. & Pamelia Stewart	No date
Pearson, Stephen & Catharine Garland	3-16-1835
Parnal, Wm. & Eliza Barnes	9-27-1835
Parish, John S. & Polly Parker	12-29-1835
Peevy, Abram & Priscilla Layfield	10-3-1837
Pinkston, Jesse M. & Hannah A. Daniel	10-18-1837
Pound, Mathew & Sarah Reeves	11-30-1837
Pierce, Joseph J. & Mary F. Howell	1-24-1838
Parmer, Dr. Etheldred & Mrs. Phoebe Ann Ashurst	5-29-1838
Peevy, Bird & Pamelia Deracken	11-29-1838
Pendleton, Dr. Edmund M. & Sara Jane Thomas	11-27-1838
Pritchett, Phillip & Martha W. Justice	12-4-1838
Parish, Thomas R. & Sarah Ann Seals	12-13-1838
Pound, David & Mary Culver	5-30-1839
Pate, Nathan & Mary G. Andrews	9-10-1839
Pitman, Matheuel & Sarah Dean, formerly Mrs. Sarah White	2-11-1840
Parker, William H. & Elizabeth Black	4-24-1840
Ponce, Francis I. & Ann Maria Richardson	12-15-1840
Pettigrew, Robert & Mary E. S. Hines	11-25-1841
Peek, John M. & Mrs. Mary West	2-23-1843
Pittman, Pathuel & Sarah Dean, formerly Mrs. Sarah White	11-8-1843
Peace, John N. & Ann Mary Minton	1-18-1844
Pound, John & Milly Ann Ellis	No date
Pound, Isaac & Julia Frances Ellis	1-24-1847
Pinkston, James M. & Anna C. Dickson	4-21-1847
Powell, Dr. Thos. Spencer & Julia Louise Bass	7-18-1847
Perdue, Reuben & Caroline Blunt	7-27-1847

Pearson, Benja Hanaford & Frances M. Whitehead	11-9-1848
Provost, Charles J. & Rebecca C. Lockhart	12-21-1848
Philpot, James & Eugenia Culver	3-11-1849
Priester, James U. & Aramintha C. Lockhart	9-16-1849
Parish, Peter & Mrs. Frances Carlisle	1-13-1850
Parker, Joseph E. & Ann Gonder	12-10-1850
Printup, E. L. & Miranda Louisa Hardwick	12-18-1850
Quinn, Thomas & Ellen Arnold	2-1-1844
Roach, Elisha & Frances Maurin	12-22-1816
Roach, William & Leah Dennis	7-7-1816
Respess, Richard & Rebecca Rogers	2-12-1806
Reid, Zepheniah & Rachel Browne	4-2-1807
Reid, Peter & Huldah Culver	9-17-1807
Richardson, James & Betsy North Clements	10-24-1807
Right, Abraham S. & Priscilla M. Rimes	1-26-1808
Reeves, Jesse T. & Patsey Murphy	8-30-1808
Richardson, Armstead & Elizabeth Peterson Grigg	9-25-1806
Reid, John & Polly Hutson	No date
Rives, George & Nancy Shackleford	No date
Rosser, Benjm & Betsy Vincent	6-1-1809
Rye, Joseph & Mary Cureton	6-29-1809
Respess, Thomas & Betsey Pritchett	12-21-1809
Rhodes, Henry & Lucy Cotton	No date
Rivers, Thomas & Polly Bonner	11-30-1809
Robertson, James & Elizabeth Thomas	1-5-1812
Rolling, Robert & Rachel Bacom	3-22-1813
Reid, Samuel D. & Eliza L. Acree	12-21-1813

Richardson, Newman & Susannah Still	2-1-1814
Rushing, William & Sarah Wilkins	6-12-1814
Randall, Edmund & Sarah H. Colquit	10-25-1814
Rives, Jesse & Sarah Jones	11-10-1814
Rudisselle, John & Mary Butler	No date
Robinson, Soloman & Mary Vickers	1-29-1815
Roberts, Benjamin & Abegail McAlister	2-7-1815
Rhodes, Lekeham & Elizabeth Henderson	8-3-1815
Reynolds, John & Jane Reynolds	5-9-1813
Ray, Thomas W. & Eliza Ellis	10-26-1815
Redding, James & Nancy H. Smith	1-9-1818
Root, David & Almira Alden	7-6-1818
Ross, David & Martha B. Wallace	7-22-1818
Ransome, Dudley & Elizabeth Roberts	8-13-1818
Rives, Henry & Sarah Vickers	12-29-1818
Rigbys, Enoch & Elizabeth Carter	5-11-1819
Reynolds, James & Susan Hester	9-23-1819
Ray, Clackston & Anna Gilmore	No date
Remington, Robert & Mary Hall	1-20-1820
Robertson, Daniel & Lucretia Sledge	No date
Ransome, Reuben & Lucy Byron	No date
Ransom, Jeremiah S. & Eanis Hester	No date
Ransom, James & Isabella Waller	No date
Reese, Jordan & Maria Saunders	1-4-1821
Reaves, Absolem E. & Eliza H. Tyus	No date
Rees, John & Ann B. Brooking	9-13-1821
Reynolds, Gabriel R. & Frances Grant	No date

Ray, James & Mary Ann Frasier	3-5-1822
Reynolds, Peter S. & Frances Grant	7-14-1822
Ridley, Archibald B. & Harriett Blackshear	12-18-1822
Rogers, Reuben & Maria R. Turner	12-31-1822
Radney, Sylvester S. & Biddy Loyd	3-6-1823
Rachels, Wm. Jr. Esq. & Elizabeth Ann Lewis Wilson	No date
Rose, David C. & Mary R. Andrews	3-25-1823
Ridley, Charles L. & Susan Ann Bonner	5-15-1823
Reynolds, Gabriel & Ann Grant	8-12-1823
Ransome, Davis & Lucinda Bird	12-27-1824
Rutland, Thomas J. & Mary Ransom	12-23-1823
Rowe, Stephen & Nancy Bird	1-19-1824
Rogers, Collin & Sarah Lawson Womack	3-21-1824
Ransom, Samuel & Eliza Garrett	8-22-1824
Ransom, Jordan D. & Emily B. Alford	6-30-1825
Richardson, Trimmakin & Roda Bartlett	10-2-1825
Roe, John Jr. & Harriett Boon	10-4-1825
Run, Lewis & Frances Worsham	10-27-1825
Ransome, John W. & Phereby Jones	11-17-1825
Reynolds, James & Mrs. Rachel Eubanks	12-25-1825
Rives, Wyatt B. & Elizabeth Gary	12-27-1825
Roberts, Burch M. & Harriett W. Hardwick	No date
Rainwater, Elisha G. & Elizabeth Grant	11-2-1826
Radney, Wm. A. & Frances Pugh	12-18-1826
Reynolds, Wm. & Sara Buckner	4-12-1827
Reese, James B. & Nancy Adams	12-30-1827
Rabun, John W. Esq. & Harriett Amanda Hagood	1-1-1828
Roach, Doctor W. & Aquilla Barefield	12-25-1827

Reaves, John & Hannah Mc Whorter	2-14-1828
Rogers, Martin D. & Eliza W. Eley	4-10-1828
Ransom, Reubin & Elizabeth Bunan	11-5-1829
Rainwater, Abner & Elizabeth Henry	No date
Ransom, Thomas S. & Susan Jackson	No date
Radney, Robert & Martha Hutchings	12-20-1831
Ransom, James B. & Sarah J. Thorp	1-5-1832
Robertson, Wm. & Mary Denton	9-13-1832
Rogers, Henry & Lucinda Dickson	12-13-1832
Rives, Irwin & Mary Colquit, formerly Mrs. Mary Cox	6-18-1833
Randall, John & Araminta Denton	3-2-1834
Roe, Jacob & Sarah Drake	No date
Radney, Benton H. & Jane B. Logue	1-1-1835
Roberts, Jared B. & Cynthia K. Evans	11-26-1835
Richardson, Richmond & Nancy S. Sherman	11-24-1835
Respess, John R. & Caroline C. Sanford	12-22-1835
Raines, John G. & Rebecca A. Kennedy	1-31-1837
Renfro, James & Mary Speights	4-2-1837
Roe, Early & Maria L. Easters	4-25-1837
Ryan, Lewis & Huldak Whitney	6-29-1837
Rowell, William & Nancy Harrison	10-25-1837
Rachel, Burwell & Lucinda Nichols	12-14-1837
Roberts, Jared B. & Martha E. Howell	1-5-1838
Russell, Behjamin & Lavenia Chambers	6-14-1838
Reynolds, John & Sarah Pounds	12-6-1838
Roberts, Franklin & Sarah Elizabeth Hudson	2-16-1840
Roach, David K. & Martha Traylor	2-13-1840

Rachel, Burwell & Mary Murphy	No date
Roberts, Charles Edward & Mary J. W. Bridges	11-22-1840
Ransom, James & Evalina Minton	3-7-1844
Roberts, James & Mrs. Arianna Watson	4-7-1846
Rogers, Benjamin F. & Elizabeth Thompson	1-2-1845
Riley, Willis & Martha Clark	12-7-1845
Rives, George S. & Susan J. Lawrence	6-30-1846
Riggins, Arthur & Elizabeth Dickens	5-16-1847
Rushin, John & Charity Trawick	No date
Rudisill, John & Ann K. Stephens	4-16-1848
Rushing, Wm. & Mrs. Mary Dabney (or Daleney)	12-26-1848
Rogers, Hezekiah & Minerva Hyman	1-25-1849
Rachels, Dickson & Sarah Ann McDaniel	No date
Ransom, Thomas H. & Amanda Phelps	11-4-1849
Rogers, Henry & Mrs. Harriett A. Hutchinson	12-20-1849
Rainwater, Simeon I & Nancy Smith	12-22-1850
Skinner, Oliver & Mary Richardson	6-21-1808
Stembridge, Wm & Elizabeth Green	6-30-1808
Shivers, William & Sally Norsworthy	5-7-
Smith, Sampson & Sophia Seales	6-23-1807
Simmons, John & Sarah Stewart	12-17-1807
Smith, David & Nancy Hay	7-31-1807
Shepheard, David & Leah Benston	9-10-
Smith, Lovet & Nancy Turk	10-1-1807
Smith, Alexander & Sarah Jeter	2-8-1808
Scott, Frederick & Polly Hudson	No date
Scott, Woodlief & Sarah Hudson	7-17-1806

Springer, William G. & Mary Baxter	No date
Southall, James & Elizabeth Wheelus	11-17-1808
Sturdivant, John & Patsy Bass	11-24-1808
Shi, Simeon & Levisa Williams	11-29-1808
Spights, John & Polly Ewing	12-8-1808
Sledge, Collins & Zelpha Harris	12-15-1808
Sollard, Edward A. & Sarah Maraton Michael	5-4-1809
Self, Hudson & Rebecca Thompson	9-12-1809
Stewart, Walter & Nancy Calloway	No date
Stewart, John & Lucinda Harry	No date
Smith, Samuel & Betsey Allen	9-19-1809
Shivers, Thomas & Eliza A. Candler	5-15-1810
Wtanton, Wm. & Nancy E. Garland	7-4-1810
Smith, Caleb & Nancy Kennedy	7-26-1810
Smith, Lemuel & Mary Dickson	11-8-1810
Shelton, Joseph & Claricy Tyson	7-24-1810
Swenney, Wilson & Polly Tyas	1-22-1811
Seales, William & Sarah Robertson	6-13-1811
Smith, Abbington F. & Mary Davis	11-27-1811
Sasnett, Joseph & Rhoda Turner	1-16-1812
Smith, John & Elizabeth Patterson	12-31-1812
Smith, John & Lucy Hamilton	12-23-1812
Smith, David & Nancy Rachels	9-16-1813
Smith, Brittain & Christian Duckworth	9-9-1813
Stembridge, Henry & Polly Bryan	11-26-1813
Slocum, Wm. & Nancy Brown	11-10-1814
Sanders, William & Elizabeth Barnes	No date

Simms, Brittain & Ann Colbert	No date
Scott, William F. & Nancy Martin	3-26-1815
Smith, Job & Nancy Norwood	7-8-1815
Stembridge, Wm. & Nancy Lewis	10-3-1815
Scott, Major Thomas B. & Mrs. Sara Jones	12-17-1815
Sykes, William & Eliza Day	12-7-1815
Swint, James & Sarah Bryant	12-14-1815
Sykes, Barnaby & Alcy Griggs	11-17-1815
Smith, John C. & Elizabeth Shivers	4-3-1816
Simpson, James & Lucretia Tucker	4-12-1816
Smith, Richard & Polly Canida	6-20-1816
Statter (or Slatter) Hope H. & Mary Tripp	9-3-1816
Simms, John & Comfort Grace	9-16-1816
Skinner, John & Turner Tarver	1-2-1817
Smith, Benjamin & Sabery Kelley	1-9-1817
Spillars, Samuel & Sarah Culver	11-26-1816
Scott, Henry F. & Rebecca Moss	12-20-1815
Sharpe, James & Elizabeth Lancaster	8-20-1817
Skinner, Manning & Mary Reynolds	12-2-1817
Styson, William & Lucindy Foster	No date
Stoval, Pleasant & Louisa R. Lucas	1-6-1818
Saxon, James H. & Eliza R. Williams	3-24-1818
Smith, William C. & Mary Moss	6-18-1818
Shivers, William Jr. & Susan F. Rabun	12-20-1818
Singer, John & Temperance Carr	10-26-1818
Shelman, John & Martha Lucas	12-22-1818
Stevens, Carlton & Cyntha Henry	1-6-1819
Sanders, John & Sarah Ferrell	No date

Sropshire, James W. & Martha Graybill	3-14-1819
Stonum, Joseph D. & Rebecca Crowder	3-18-1819
Smith, James & Eunice Miles	8-12-1819
Swint, William & Anna Bryant	1-20-1820
Shivers, John M. & Sarah A. Hamilton	11-3-1819
Smith, Calvin & Priscilla Eubanks	4-13-1820
Shivers, Jonas & Martha M. Denson	2-3-1821
Smith, Horace & Jane W. Horton	2-10-1821
Simmons, Thomas & Elenor Benson	No date
Slaughter, Thomas P. & Mary Stembridge	3-6-1821
Simmerson, Asa & Mrs. Marcella Goodwin	6-14-1821
Standley, Samuel & Martha Brown	10-23-1821
Stephens, Jacob & Mildred Thompson	4-11-1822
Slaton, John & Ann Harris	10-24-1822
Smith, William & Elizabeth Warren	12-31-1822
Smith, Thomas A. & Mrs. Eliza J. Fraser	1-1-1823
Scott, John W. & Harriet Hall	2-16-1823
Stowers, Jesse & Sarah Reese	No date
Snipes, William B. & Sarah Jane Sheffield	No date
Shivers, Obediah J. & Sarah Long	12-9-1823
Shelman, Robert B. Esq. & Caroline L. Lucas	1-22-1824
Stewart, Frederick S. & Naomi J. Rhea	2-19-1824
Schley, Phillip T. & Frances V. L. Brooking	7-8-1824
Stephens, Wm. B. & Pamelia S. Turner	5-24-1825
Spillers, Samuel & Martha Culver	7-24-1825
Simmons, Dudley & Melinda Dennis	9-15-1825
Slayton, Joseph & Synthia Drake	11-1-1825
Sanders, Thomas J. & Hunty Griggs	12-15-1825

Staples, Sophos Esq. & Sarah Abercrombie formerly Mrs. Sarah Harris	1-10-1826
Stewart, Lorenza Sneed & Signa Ora Whitehead	1-24-1826
Saunders, Lovett & Martha Barksdale	12-19-1826
Stokes, Archibald & Catharine Paton	2-15-1827
Saunders, James H. & Rebecca Franklin	5-17-1827
Smith, John P. & Louisa C. Broad	8-8-1827
Sykes, John P. & Nancy B. Brown	10-9-1827
Smith, Hezekiah & Areanna Smith	10-24-1827
Smith, Otis & Martha M. Womack	12-11-1827
Spillers, John & Matilda Culver	12-23-1827
Smith, Aaron & Mary J. Miller	2-17-1828
Smith, Wilkins & Mrs. Rebecca Harris	1-22-1828
Sherman, Robert H. & Martha Lancaster	2-12-1828
Shackleford, Edmund & Mrs. Mary Hagood	1-11-1829
Sheffield, William & Mary Sheffield	1-13-1829
Smith, Hardy & Lucretia Miller	2-17-1829
Simms, Benjamin C. & Adeline D. Wright	No date
Smith, Robert M. & Priscilla Parker	10-8-1829
Smith John E. & Mary S. Hudson	12-1-1829
Simmons, Richard & Mrs. Rebecca Buttington	12-13-1829
Stanley, Spirus & Nancy Thompson	1-10-1830
Stephens, Enoch & Susannah Brown	4-11-1830
Skinner, Alfred & Mrs. Nancy Skinner	7-1-1830
Sheppard, John & Phanetty Watkins	9-9-1830
Seals, James W. & Nancy W. Seals	10-20-1831
Seales, Spencer & Rebecca Culverhouse	12-7-1831
Smith, James & Penelope Stanford	12-8-1831

lerk
re-
ved

Strother, Richard & Mary Black	2-23-1832
Smith, Marshall & Temperance Sorrel	4-1-1832
Street, Wm. B. Esq. & Eliza L. Beman	5-24-1832
Shivers, Barnaby Esq. & Mrs. Sarah H. Gregory	9-5-1832
Seymore, Willborn W. & Eliza L. Eubanks	10-19-1832
Simmons, James W. & Catharine L. Butts	11-14-1833
Switzer, Edwin & Louisa Turner	3-6-1834
Scott, John E. & Mary M. Sharpe	4-8-1834
Simmons, John B. & Everlina A. Roe	5-13-1834
Simmons, John T. & Ann Pugh	12-22-1834
Smith, William C. & Maria S. Butts	2-5-1836
Shearman, Edwin T. & Priscilla Turner	3-3-1836
Stewart, James & Mrs. Margaret Stewart	4-27-1836
Simpson, Felix & Mary McLelen	11-1-1836
Simpson, Jacob W. & Catharine S. Cook	12-8-1836
Smith, James D. & Minerva C. Powell	12-11-1836
Sanford, Benjamin F. & Sarah A. R. Choice	12-29-1836
Swinney, John L. & Julia Maria Tomlinson	12-19-1837
Smith, Andrew J. & Ann C. Scuddy	2-5-1838
Smith, George W. & Alzada S. Binion	4-17-1838
Sanders, Abram & Anna Scoals	9-12-1838
Smith, Samuel & Rebecca Osborn	10-23-1838
Shivers, John M. & Mildred Sheffield	1-27-1839
Speights, Wm. H. & Mary Ann Atkins	6-11-1839
Scott, Thomas R. & Elizabeth R. Speights	12-18-1838
Shaffer, Joseph L. Esq. & Henrietta M. Bonner	12-12-1839
Sacher, Minnis & Margaret Wilcoxen	12-15-1839
Smith, Major Lovitt S. & Sarah Lurana Cook	1-28-1841

Shivers, William & Mrs. Sarah Ann Beddo	3-30-1841
Smith, James & Mahala Jane Johnson	6-3-1841
Smith, Joel & Mary Rebecca Caldwell	10-19-1841
Scott, James H. & Mary E. Mitchell	12-15-1841
Sanford, Frederick H. & Evelina Rosa Brooking	12-30-1841
Smith, Theophilus J. & Mary S. Gonder	No date
Stokes, Rev. William & Mrs. Melissa Jane Evans	8-18-1842
Simpson, Jeptha & Nicey Chambers	3-19-1843
Smith, Rev. Osborn L. & Amanda Lawrence	12-12-1843
Smith, William C. & Martha A. D. Burton	1-25-1844
Shivers, Columbus F. & Eliza Ann Latimer	6-20-1844
Stephens, Jacob & Eliza Blizzard	No date
Simmons, Marcellus A. & Mary Amanda Melvina Jackson	3-18-1846
Smith, Harrison & Mary Gladding	8-27-1846
Simpson, James R. & Mary A. Harris	9-15-1846
Skrine, John J. & Elizabeth J. Powell	12-31-1846
Sharp, James L. & Delany Hill	2-25-1847
Soullard, James A. & Cornelia A. Smith	8-2-1847
Stewart, Lorenza S. Esq. & Wlizabeth B. Whitehead	8-24-1847
Storey, Richard L. & Jane C. Dickson	10-27-1847
Smith, Thomas & Martha Johnson	9-17-1848
Smith, Henry D. & Nancy D. Rudisill	11-9-1848
Starling, Mills & Rebecca Rachels	3-4-1849
Smith, George G. & Emily F. Evans	11-22-1849
Smith, John E. & Emily Johnson	1-6-1850
Smith, John E. & Emily Johnson	1-6-1850
Springs, A. Baxter & Blandina Baxter	2-12-1850
Stanford, James M. & Elizabeth A. Sykes	4-30-1850

Summerrell, Clinton & Nancy Jordan   9-15-1850

Turner, Levin & Ellendar   12-18-1806

Tiler, Thomas & Sarah Shi   2-26-1807

Turner, Henry & Sally Evans   6-12-1807

Turner, Samuel & Sarah Roe   7-2-1807

Thweatt, Thomas & Temperance Seegars Surner   10-13-1807

Tilman, John & Sally Wadsworth   9-10-1807

Traywick, Jesse & Elizabeth Barrow   3-3-1808

Thomas, Harrison & Silvey Wallace   4-3-1806

Travis, Whitmell & Allah Thompson   12-8-1808

Tatum, Peter & Nancy Sledge   No date

Traywick, John & Patsy Hitchcock   4-24-1810

Templin, Charles & Polly Bishop   No date

Turner, Samuel & Betsy Bynum   2-12-1811

Talley, Peyton & Polly Buckner   4-4-1811

Turner, Jacob P. & Nancy Lundy   1-15-1812

Tool, David & Elizabeth Evans   2-10-1811

Tally, Wm. & Susannah Owens   7-16-1812

Thompson, James & Polly J. Holt   7-15-1812

Traywick, Robert & Susannah Hitchcock   9-3-1812

Tyus, Joshua & Polly Chappell   12-22-1812

Thermon, Stephen & Eliza Harvey   3-18-1813

Turner, George & Elizabeth Culver   5-28-1813

Turner, Jacob & Polly Saunders   12-14-1813

Tyson, Aaron & Jane Brown Lucas   4-14-1814

Thornton, John & Sally Griggs   6-5-1814

Tilman, James & Elinor Riddle	11-17-1814
Turner, Elisha P. & Nancy Ross	11-15-1814
Townsend, Thomas & Elenor Thomas	No date
Turner, Benjamin & Rebecca Echols	4-13-1815
Tidd, David & Polly Cagle	5-25-1815
Traywick, John H. & Elizabeth Fason	4-4-1816
Traywick, George & May Gary	6-9-1816
Turner, Henry & Jane Cozart	9-17-1816
Thornton, James & Nancy Butts	10-3-1816
Tyus, Lewis & Mary Hall	No date
Thresh, Ely & Frances Butler	11-22-1816
Tilman, John Jr. & Mary White	12-29-1816
Tidd, Joseph & Catharine Cagle	12-29-1816
Thompson, Henry T. & Nancy Owens	10-9-1817
Taylor, Ozias & Lerena Spights	1-22-1818
Taylor, Swisston & Sarah Mitchell	2-11-1818
Trippe, Henry & Martha Ingram	2-12-1818
Tucker, Jacob & Elizabeth Warren	2-4-1819
Turner, James S. & Penelope Simms	4-26-1819
Tilly, George & Sarah Simms	12-23-1819
Thomas, Mark Smith & Sarah Shivers	11-4-1819
Thompson, James & Lutiney Ewing	3-3-1820
Thomas, James Esq. & Emily M. Gonder	No date
Thweatt, Thomas & Catharine A. S. Hamill	8-28-1821
Thomas, Grigsby E. & Mary A. Shivers	10-16-1821

Tait, Honbl. Charles & Mrs. Sarah Griffin   5-1-1822

Thomason, Thomas & Nancy Holmes   10-3-1822

Turner, John & Susan S. Dickinson   12-14-1822

Thomas, John R. & Rebecca Brantley   1-8-1823

Tarver, Andrew & Mrs. Nancy S. Colquitt   7-16-1823

Tyus, William G. & Maria J. Thomas   8-21-1823

Tarver, Benjamin & Priscilla N. Eley   8-28-1823

Thompson, Joseph & Aspey Minton   11-6-1823

Turner, Mathew & Mary Ann Eliza Thomas   1-8-1824

Thomas, Samuel B. & Ann R. Askey   1-25-1825

Thomas, James O. B. & Mary B. Tyus   10-15-1825

Tillmon, Burgess & Charity Parker   12-14-1825

Turner, John & Elizabeth C. Askew   1-17-1826

Turner, Wm. T. & Sarah Grant   9-26-1826

Tolson, Henry & Levina Smith   12-26-1826

Taylor, Simon M. & Eliza Andrews   1-23-1827

Thomas, Doctor W. & Phoebe H. Gilbert   1-11-1827

Thompson, Israel & Lucy Peek   9-13-1827

Thomas, Thomas & Louizer Griffin   9-30-1827

Thornton, Harrison & Matilda Benson   4-13-1828

Thompson, John & Elizabeth Frances Haynes   4-30-1828

Twiss, Thomas S. & Elizabeth Shurill   7-13-1828

Tyus, Wm. G. & Rebecca J. Culver   5-20-1829

Trawick, George R. & Sarah Purvis   8-4-1829

Thornton, John & Mary M. Pettigrew   11-5-1829

Thompson, Wm. B. & Sarah E. Huff   11-17-1829

Timmons, Richard & Mrs. Rebecca Buttington   12-13-1829

Trawick, Francis & Lucy Johnson   9-9-1830

Thomas, Edwin C. J. B. & Mary Ann Gilbert   11-20-1831

Taylor, Henry L. & Mary Ann Lucas   4-4-1833

Taylor, Wm. & Maria L. Brooking   5-28-1834

Tamplin, Reubin & Mary Thorington   3-17-1836

Turner, Jonathon & Polly Jones   11-24-1836

Taylor, James & Elizabeth Meeks   12-18-1836

Thornton, Andrew Jackson & Elizabeth Susan Clarke   No date

Trippe, James I. & Melinda Griggs   9-14-1837

Turner, Mathew & Artemesa W. Cato   12-14-1837

Turner, Thomas M. & Sarah R. Clayton   12-12-1837

Trawick, Thomas J. & Bertha E. Dickson   10-24-1838

Tyus, William G. & Mary Jackson   4-19-1840

Tate, Joseph L. & Martha Bartlett   9-8-1844

Turner, Martillus Drumman & Mrs. Caroline Eliza Lucas   3-10-1846

Thorpe, Dr. Joseph B. & Mary M. Griggs   9-13-1846

Trawick, Moses W. & Lithe Ann Osborne   1-11-1846

Terry, James & Sarah Talley   2-22-1847

Turner, Riley M. & Frances P. Garrett   2-25-1847

Thornton, John & Mary A. Gordy   12-29-1847

Thomas, Gabriel R. & Judy Ann Fears   9-4-1848

Taylor, John & Mrs. Elizabeth Ray   12-20-1848

Thompson, Mathew & Susan Judkins   No date

Turner, Alexander Washington & Elizabeth McCoy   3-7-1850

Turner, John B. & Caroline M. Hardwick   11-19-1850

Underwood, Lawson & Caroline Barksdale	11-23-1831
Upchurch, Abner F. & Lucinda Upchurch	1-27-1832
Underwood, William & Sarah Jane Peeler	11-26-1846
Veazey, Ezekial & Rachel Stewart	10-30-1806
Vinson, Isaac & Polly Kanady	2-1-1807
Vinson, Davis & Alis Smith	5-25-1809
Vickers, Thomas & Marian Armstrong	1-29-1811
Vinson, Selby & Ann Middlebrooks	3-4-1812
Valley, George & Lurany Smith	5-6-1813
Veazey, Stephen & Nancy Weeks	12-8-1813
Vickers, Wm. & Mary Ray	12-29-1814
Veazey, Jesse & Leah W. Hall	2-13-1817
Veazey, Alanson E. & Cynthia Reynolds	1-9-1823
Voicle, Josiah & Sytha Conner	2-27-1825
Vinson, Wesley Esq. & Sarah Ann Eubanks	5-9-1836
Veal, Jourdan & Mrs. Martha Wagers	2-5-1838
Veal, Edward & Martha Ann Chambers	10-7-1838
Vinson, Levin & Mary Ann H. Garey	1-12-1842
Williams, Thomas & Patsy Powell	9-7-1806
Wall, Arthur & Nancy Bowman	2-2-1807
Wilkerson, Abner & Nelly Dent	3-13-1807
Willis, James & Marthy Murphey	10-11-1807
Waller, Loxla & Nella Dent	1-28-1808
Weltshem, Duke Wm. & Mary Allen	3-17-1808
Walters, Phillimon & Peggy Lee	No date
Webb, John & Sarah Moon	9-18-1806
Wallace, Abraham & Phebe Carr	4-17-1810

Wadsworth, Sidney & Betsey Tait	5-6-1810
Williams, Abraham & Sarah Culver	6-14-1810
Waller, Zepheniah & Gatty Layfield	5-24-1812
Wilkinson, Adam & Nancy Hall	9-17-1812
Whaley, Samuel & Marian Kelly	11-11-1812
Williams, Jehu & Sarah Dismukes	12-17-1812
Weaver, Cordy & Polly Pope	12-15-1812
Waller, Joseph & Polly Dent	2-17-1813
Williamson, Wyatt & Hannah Brown	9-12-1813
Wyley, Isaac & Ann M. Thompson	5-19-1813
West, John & Mary Sanford	No date
Watson, Richard L. & Jane Birch	11-15-1814
Webb, John & Nancy Thomison	3-29-1815
Williams, Wm. & Sarah Mathews	6-11-1815
Waller, Ellis & Caroline Broadnax	6-6-1815
Wethersby, George M. & Sarah Speight	11-26-1815
Wilkerson, James & Priscilla Davis	12-7-1815
Whittington, John & Nancy E. Harris	1-11-1816
Wright, Elliott & Eleanor Hobbs	2-23-1816
Watson, Wm. C. & Sarah S. Peterson	11-5-1816
Williams, John & Tinna Morgan	11-4-1816
Wright, Abednego & Susannah Gairy	11-7-1816
Wynne, Burwell & Gillah Ann Sanders	12-3-1816
White, Frederick & Ruth Fulsom	No date
Wooten, James & Ann Butler	8-7-1817
Wright, Sampson & Margaret Hall	9-2-1817
White, Daniel & Martha Blount	9-25-1817
Wiley, Edwin & Eliza Dewett	10-7-1817
Whittington, John & Mary Ann Traywick	4-30-1815

Weatherly, Arvis & Dicy Mathers	4-14-1818
White, Willie & Frances Ann Gary	6-4-1818
Wilson, Robert & Mary Osborn	7-9-1818
Waller, James & Polly Arnold	10-4-1818
Wilson, James & Caty Ozbun	10-22-1818
Womack, Wiley & Emily Byrom	12-15-1818
Worthin, Elijah & Elizabeth Thomas	1-28-1819
Wooton, James A. & Susannah B. Byrom	2-11-1819
Wilcox, Cyprian & Catherine De Witt	5-4-1819
Woodard, Isham & Mary P. Williams	No date
Wright, Flewellin & Frances M. Goode	11-25-1819
Whitehead, Bird & Nancy C. Tucker	11-23-1819
Waller, Benjamin & Celia Crimean	1-27-1820
Warn, Richard & Julia Pierpont	6-5-1820
Wood, Rev. W. Joseph & Mary Warner Doly	1-7-1821
Williamson, Thomas C. &	No date
Walker, John & Mary Tyus (Mrs.)	4-17-1821
Warthen, Elijah & Hannah Dureton	No date
Wheeler, James & Martha Cummins	5-23-1822
Waller, John & Elizabeth Griggs	8-15-1822
Wayne, Greene & Margaret W. Lewis	9-24-1822
White, William M. & Rebecca Cordall	12-12-1822
Warthen, William B. & Melinda Dickson	2-20-1823
Willcoxen, Levi & Linnah Griggs	2-6-1823
Worsham, William & Frances Wagby	3-12-1823
Wilkinson, Benjamin & Elizabeth Tillman	1-1-1824
Welkins, Wilkinson & Nancy Gardner	2-12-1824

Williams, John & Elizabeth Cureton	8-10-1824
Worsham, Mitchell & Matilda Dennis	8-12-1824
Wadsworth, John & Nancy Wadsworth	12-31-1824
Wade, Hamlin L. & Sybbel Parker	No date
Wright, Abednigo A. & Sarah P.C.S.Wade	1-15-1825
Wright, James N. & Catherine Wade	2-13-1825
Wynn, Gabriel & Jemima W. Palmer	9-29-1825
Wilson, Dr. Josiah N. & Eliza J. Battle	10-13-1825
Wilkins, James & Elizabeth Hall	1-5-1826
Woodward, John L. & Sarah Hunt	12-25-1826
Williams, Littleberry A. & Amanda A. Cato	5-16-1827
Walker, John H. & Emily H. Brown	6-19-1827
Walker, David & Elizabeth Talbert	7-19-1827
Walker, Clement & Clary W. Cato	4-17-1828
Williford, Wiley & Mrs. Sarah Robertson	No date
Warthen, Green & Martha Thompson	6-11-1828
Williams, William Esq. & Dimmis C. P. Broad	No date
Welch, Daniel & Angelina Cureton	No date
Wagner, Benjamin & Amanda H. Borland	12-24-1829
White, John D. & Nancy Ewing	7-7-1830
White, Robert W. & Mary E. Seales	1-24-1830
Wooten, John R. Esq.& Julissey E. Trawick	No date
Warren, Eppes W. & Elizabeth Smith	No date
White, George & Delpha Barnes	No date
Waller, Zephaniah & Nancy Jean	No date
Wilcoxen, John & Mary Ann Bass	12-22-1831
Ward, John M. & Martha W. Brodnax	3-22-1832
Welch, Daniel & Charlotte Culver	10-6-1833

Walker, Minor Esq. & Martha K. B. Peterson	11-20-1833
Wells, Wm. & Mary E. Scott	12-17-1833
Wheeler, Elbert & Lucy F. Thompson	No date
White, James L. & Martha Howell	2-2-1834
White, Bailey & Cynthia Youngblood	2-19-1834
Warren, Jesse M. & Ann L. Horton	4-34-1834
Warthen, James M. & Lurana Dickson	8-21-1834
Wright, George & Lucinda Carlile	9-26-1835
Williams, Joseph & Mary Shy	1-21-1836
White, John & Sarah Dean	No date
Warren, Jesse M. & Mary Breedlove	11-17-1836
Wright, Thomas & Sarah Carlile	3-38-1837
Wilcoxen, James & Adaline Binion	No date
Whitehead, Isaac P. Esq. & Eliza Denton	12-7-1837
Watts, William & Nancy Hall	12-13-1838
Wheeler, Henry C. & Helen C. Milliner	No date
Whitehead, Nelson & Sarah A. E. Trippe	1-13-1839
Waller, Zephaniah & Elizabeth Carlisle	2-3-1839
Waller, Jeptha & Priscilla Ellis	5-7-1839
Welch, Charles B. & Marian Wilson	6-11-1839
Waller, Irwin & Martha Williams	10-8-1839
Wood, Robert T. & Mary Thornton	12-10-1839
Whaley, James R. & Martha Ann Walker	12-10-1840
Whitehead, Charles E. & Julia C. Burnet	6-8-1841
Walker, John Edward & Luverna Elizabeth Culver	11-17-184?
Ware, David R. & Martha Ann Buckner	8-17-1843
Winslow, Elbridge & Rebecca H. Smith	1-4-1844

Wilcoxen, James & Adaline A. Grace	3-19-1844
Wilkins, Archibald & Florida Mitchell	11-10-1846
Wilson, Benja J. & Caroline S. Cheely	5-26-1847
Williams, Abram M. & Mary Ann Knowles	1-27-1848
Waller, John & Frances F. Brodnax	3-5-1848
Whaley, Thomas & Mary Morris	3-23-1848
Warthen, Wm. & Applewhite H. Griggs	1-8-1850
Wilson, Shepherd & Isabel Layfield	12-5-1850
Young, Amos & Nancy Bailey	8-20-1807
Youngblood, John & Betsy Fuller	10-15-1807
Youngblood, James & Nancy Kennedy	9-8-1812
Youngblood, Abraham & Amey Smith	12-28-1815
Youngblood, William L. & Elizabeth Youngblood	9-9-1816
Youngblood, Isaac R. & Elizabeth Kennedy	No date
Young, Enos & Sylvia L. Tarver	3-20-1817
Young, Henry & Mary Warren	3-23-1817
Yarbrough, Isaac & Jane McDaniel	2-14-1822
Youngblood, Joseph & Phoebe Waller	11-6-1823
Youngblood, Isaac & Melvina Kennan	7-28-1834
Yeates, Peter & Mary Ann Turner	12-3-1837
Yancey, Benjamin C. Esq. & Laura M. Hines	7-20-1841
Young, George W. & Sarah Hood	1-5-1842
Yates, James E. & Elizabeth P. Jordan	6-11-1844
Youngblood, George W. & Margaret V. Lewis	1-11-1847
Zackry, Abner J. & America Ann Culver	8-29-1850